MOZART

SOME REFLECTIONS

Mozart is the most inaccessible
of the great masters.

Artur Schnabel

TABLE OF CONTENTS

INTRODUCTION

Wolfgang Amadeus Mozart was not only one of the greatest composers of the Classical period, but one of the greatest of all time. Surprisingly, he is not identified with radical formal or harmonic innovations, or with the profound kind of symbolism heard in some of Bach's works. Mozart's best music has a natural flow and irresistible charm, and can express humor, joy or sorrow with both conviction and mastery. His operas, especially his later efforts, are brilliant examples of high art, as are many of his piano concertos and later symphonies. Even his lesser compositions and juvenile works feature much attractive and often masterful music.

He was born in Salzburg, Austria on January 27, 1756. His parents, Leopold and Anna Maria Mozart, named him Johannes Chrysostomus Wolfgangus Gottlieb Mozart. He was one of seven children born to the couple, but only Wolfgang (his popular name) and an older sister, Maria Anna (called Marianne and nicknamed "Nannerl" - born July 30, 1751) survived past infancy.

Leopold Mozart had dropped out of university in order to pursue a career in music, and at the time of Wolfgang's birth he was employed with the court orchestra at Augsburg. The Mozart family was a tightly bonded unit, and it was within the family unit that Mozart would achieve most of the fame he received in his lifetime.

Leopold decided that he would take on the education of his children himself, and he concentrated on musical instruction. He was well pleased to realize that both of his offspring were gifted musicians, and began to see it as his God-given responsibility to guide them into a performing life. Mozart first picked up an instrument at age three, when he took an interest in the clavier his sister was learning and began to pick out notes and rhythms on his own.

Much of the true biography of Mozart has been written and deduced through the correspondence of both himself and his family. In one such letter, Leopold Mozart reflected to a friend late in life that he had perhaps made his children don the "iron shirt of discipline" too tightly.

Despite the regrets of an aging parent, the methods that Leopold undertook to educate his progeny cannot be said to have been anything but effective. Wolfgang learned his first musical composition, a *Scherzo* by Gorg Christoph Wagenseil, days before he turned five, and in half an hour. He wrote his own first composition at five, a six measure andante in C Major. Between the ages of five and nine, Wolfgang would write 30 compositions. By the time he was 20 years old, he had completed 219.

Before the flowering of his prolific gifts, though, the young Wolfgang was to be exposed to the musical influences that he would so often remember and incorporate into his own writing. He was given this opportunity when his father, realizing the talents of his children needed to be known, and also taking advantage of the possibilities for the family purse, decided to take Wolfgang and Maria on tour to Vienna. This tour turned out to be groundbreaking, as noble household after noble household heard the children play and walked away amazed. Word soon spread throughout Austria of the prodigies, and the Mozarts found themselves performing before the Emperor and Empress at the Schonbrunn Palace. A young Wolfgang displayed all the innocent exuberance of childhood when he climbed up into the Empress' lap.

After this performance, the Mozarts were in high demand throughout the district. Leopold would book performance after performance, both publicly and for private noble households. The children were usually called upon to perform two concerts a day. The group's first major publicist, Baron Friedrich Melchior Grimm, stated that watching Wolfgang play was "[...] such an extraordinary phenomenon that one is hard put to believe what one sees with one's eyes and hears with one's ears". The Mozarts continued to tour throughout Europe, and when a serious illness (which he believed would be the end of him) took Leopold, the tours came to a pause. During this time, Wofgang wrote his first symphony for all the instruments of an orchestra. He flourished during this break, and wrote two more symphonies before his father recovered and they again went on the road. He was eight years old.

The illness that affected his father was not a new occurrence among the Mozarts. The whole family was prone to sickness, and Wolfgang had been severely sick several times since embarking on the tours. Both he and his sister were so sick at times that their parents gave up on them as lost, and summoned a priest to read them their last rites.

Mozart wrote his first opera, *La Finta Semplice*, at the age of 12. Between 14 and 17 the Mozarts made three trips to Italy, where Mozart learned the Italian style of composing and incorporated it into his operas *Mitridate, re di Ponto* and *Lucio Silla*.

At 18, he began working as Kozertmeister at the Prince-Archbishop's court in Salzburg, where he wrote masses, symphonies, all of his violin concertos, six piano sonatas, several serenades, and his first great piano concerto, K271.

When Wolfgang turned 21, his family began to look for arenas where his extremely advanced skills as a composer could flourish, instead of remaining in the stifling environment of Salzburg. As usual, the Mozarts did their traveling together, but on a trip to Paris in 1778 Wolfgang's mother died with a feverish illness. Two years later, Wofgang Mozart was summoned to Vienna where he wrote the opera *Idomeneo*. Despite the success of this work, however, Mozart felt that his time in Vienna was wasted in the employ of the Prince-Archbishop Colloredo, and they parted ways in sullen fashion, Mozart saying in a letter to his sister that he departed "with a kick in the seat of the pants".

Mozart continued his musical career as a freelancer. He taught music, gave performances, and composed by commission. In 1782, he began concentrating on his piano concertos, in order that he could appear as both composer and soloist. In four years, he completed 15 pieces. Mozart also married Constance Weber in 1782, to the consternation of his father. The marriage caused a rift that was never to be closed, and despite the couple's visits and attempts to reconcile, Leopold Mozart died in 1787 never fully happy with the union.

In the year of his father's death, Mozart was the composer of the Imperial and Royal Chamber, which paid a salary of 800fl a year. His work was not popular among his native provinces, but he had begun to gain fame throughout the rest of Europe. The new popularity did not translate into wealth, however, as there were neither performance rights nor copyright laws at this time. Ironically, Mozart only began seeing the returns from the massive impact his compositions were having on the rest of Europe in 1791, the year of his death, as publishers began to pay for the rights to publish his works. Mozart died on

December 5, 1791; he left behind a son, Karl Thomas (born in 1784) and a pregnant Constance. Both his sons would go on to become composers, and Franz Xaver Süssmayr, one of his students, would complete Mozart's *Requiem*, left unfinished upon his death.

Mozart's contributions to the musical landscape are irrefutable. Haydn described him as "the greatest composer known to me in person or by name; he has taste and, what is more, the greatest knowledge of composition". The influence of his work on their own art was readily acknowledged by many composers. Beethoven wrote four such sets (Op. 66, WoO 28, WoO 40, WoO 46). Others include Frédéric Chopin's Variations on "*Là ci darem la mano*" from *Don Giovanni* (1827); Max Reger's Variations and Fugue on a Theme by Mozart (1914), based on the variation theme in the Piano sonata K. 331; Fernando Sor's Introduction and Variations on a Theme by Mozart (1821); and Mikhail Glinka's Variations on a Theme from Mozart's opera *Die Zauberflöte* (1822). Pyotr Ilyich Tchaikovsky wrote his Orchestral Suite No. 4 in G (1887), more commonly known as *Mozartiana*.

THE MOZART EFFECT

Music affects us all! Its powerful effects are fundamental in life, and its beneficiaries always appear to perform better in life. We sing with it and dance to it. We accompany our most important rituals with music. We sing hymns to our Gods and pen anthems for our nations. There is no culture in the history of mankind that has not had music.

Most of the greatest minds in history were musicians, or compelled music's power. Einstein, one of the most brilliant minds in history was a violinist, and admitted that one of the reasons why he was so smart was because he played the violin. He found solutions to complex equations and problems by improvising on the violin. When Thomas Jefferson couldn't find the correct wording for a passage in the Declaration of Independence, he played his violin, and found the correct wording. Music helped him to project the words from mind to paper. Conan Doyle made his superlative character, Sherlock Holmes, play the violin when he was to solve a particularly complex case. Great men of history, from Shakespeare to Napoleon were in some way dedicated to music, and this is what made the difference: music.

Science has always tried to explain music, to tell us why and how it affects us so. Because music's influence is so subjective and the brain is so poorly understood, this subject is especially susceptible to myths and exaggerations.

On this premise, this chapter analyzes the so called 'Mozart effect', the idea that passively listening to the music of this composer can make a person smarter.

The 'Mozart effect' was first suggested in 1991 by Alfred Angelo Tomatis (1920 - 2001), a French otolaryngology researcher, in his book, *Pourquoi Mozart*? Originally called "The Tomatis Effect", the phenomenon dealt with human hearing as a cognitive process that goes beyond the mere sensory phenomenon and suggested that listening to Mozart could have effects on cognitive brain regions in addition to the more obvious sensory brain networks (a very useful support in case of dyslexia, autism, other learning disorders and depression).

Early experimentation on the effect of music on the brain was conducted in 1988, when neuroscientist Gordon Shaw, along with graduate student Xiaodan Leng, first attempted to model brain activity on a computer at the University of California at Irvine (Center for the Neurobiology of Learning and Memory). They found in simulations that the way nerve cells were connected to one another predisposed groups of cells to adopt certain specific firing patterns and rhythms. Shaw surmises that these patterns form the basic exchange of mental activity. Inquisitively, they decided to turn the output of their simulations into sounds instead of a conventional printout. To their surprise, the rhythmic patterns sounded somewhat familiar, with some of the characteristics of baroque, new age, or Eastern music.

If brain activity can sound like music, Shaw hypothesized, might it be possible to begin to understand the neural activity by working in reverse and observing how the brain responds to music? Might patterns in music somehow stimulate the brain by activating similar firing patterns of nerve clusters?

The real explosion in the popularity of this concept came in 1993 when Shaw joined researcher Katherine Ky and Frances Rauscher, a former concert cellist and an expert on cognitive development. In the October 14 1993 issue of *Nature* magazine, UC Irvine researchers published a short, one-page article entitled

"Music and Spatial Task Performance: A Casual Relationship". The article — presented at the American Psychological Association 102nd Annual Convention (Los Angeles, CA August 12-16, 1994) — highlighted that well-developed spatial intelligence is the ability to perceive the visual world accurately, to form mental images of physical objects, and to recognize variations of objects. The researchers theorized that spatial reasoning abilities are crucial for such higher brain functions as music, complex mathematics, and chess. As many of the problems in which scientists and engineers engage in cannot be described in verbal form, progress in science may, in fact, be closely linked to the development of certain spatial skills.

Rauscher, Shaw, and Ky reported that 36 undergraduates increased their mean spatial-reasoning scores the equivalent of 8 to 9 IQ points on portions of the Stanford-Binet Intelligence Scale: Fourth Edition (Thorndike, Hagen, & Sattler, 1986) after listening to 10 min of Mozart's Sonata for Two Pianos in D Major, K. 448. The effect was temporary, having disappeared within 10 to 15 min.

Subsequently, Rauscher, Shaw, and Ky (1995) reported a replication of the 'Mozart effect', using elaborations of the Stanford-Binet Paper Folding and Cutting (S-B PF&C) task as the dependent measure. The hypothesis that musical experiences of short duration can have a direct causal influence on spatial reasoning on both a short-term and a long-term basis (Rauscher, 1997) is important for both practical and theoretical reasons.

Rauscher and Shaw (1998) reviewed some of the negative results and described key components necessary to produce a 'Mozart effect'. Negative results in some studies were explained by the choice of an inappropriate dependent measure, and the use of a PF&C task was endorsed. Rauscher and Shaw warned investigators to attend to issues concerning the order of presentation of the listening and task conditions. A major concern was that a pretest immediately before the treatment may produce a carryover effect that obscures enhancement by the music. The purpose of this experiment was to confirm the existence of the 'Mozart effect' by following the advice of Rauscher and Shaw (1998).

The experiment was designed to be a faithful replication of the central conditions of the Rauscher *et al.* (1995) experiment. Scholars tested the effect of exposure to Mozart's Sonata for Two Pianos (K.448) against silence and against highly repetitive music (Philip Glass's Music with Changing Parts) in a mixed-groups design. They chose to replicate the 1995 experiment because more procedural details were available for that experiment than for the earlier experiment, because the overall magnitude of the 'Mozart effect' was stronger in the 1995 experiment, and because the procedure was consistent with the recommendations of Rauscher and Shaw (1998).

Again, the group that listened to the Mozart selection showed an increase in spatial IQ test scores. A further test showed that listening to other types of music (non-specified "dance" music) did not have the same effect.

Rauscher *et al.* (1995) employed 79 participants, distributed among three conditions. This study involved 125 participants (42 male and 83 female) distributed among three conditions.

Participants came from introductory psychology courses and received credit for participation. Researchers used several sets of 16 Paper Folding and Cutting items (hereafter shortened to PF&C) that were derived from the Stanford-Binet IQ measure. (The actual test contains 2 practice items and 18 test items.)

They used two sets of 16 PF&C items; each set was composed approximately of half derived items and half true items from the Stanford-Binet measure. The PF&C sets were of approximately equal difficulty and had been developed in another laboratory (Rideout & Laubach, 1996). Each PF&C item was adjusted in size to occupy the center portion of an overhead transparency measuring 21.5 by 28 cm.

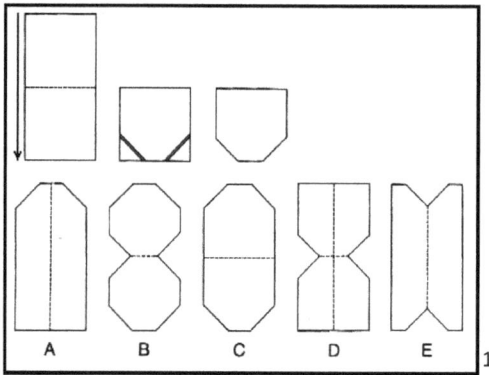

---

[1] Practice Stanford-Binet Paper Folding and Cutting item. The top row shows a piece of paper undergoing a series of transformations from left to right. The dotted line indicates the location of a fold; double lines indicate the location of cuts. The task is to pick the illustration in the bottom row that represents the appearance of the transformed paper when it is unfolded. For the item illustrated here, the correct answer is "C".

Stimulus tapes were created from the CD performances used in Rauscher *et al.*. Mozart's Sonata for Two Pianos, K. 448 is a lively three-movement piece. Although invariably described as 10 min in duration, the first section (Allegro con spirito) is actually 8 minutes, 24 seconds in duration in this performance. Philip Glass's Music With Changing Parts is more than 60 min in duration without break; the first 8 min, 24 sec was recorded for use in the experiment. The Glass composition eschews a traditional melody and uses repetition of units. The units are often only a few seconds long, and the repetition often lasts for several minutes. Exposure to music is an established mood-induction technique, and musical selections by Mozart have been used to induce a mood of elation (Kenealy, 1997; Westerman, Spies, Stahl, & Hesse, 1996).

It has been suggested that the performance difference interpreted as evidence of a 'Mozart effect' could be produced indirectly through differences in mood or arousal among treatments (Steele *et al.*, 1997). Researchers therefore used a mood measure to investigate this possibility. Individuals described the Mozart selection as "lively," "bouncy," and "happy"; the same individuals described the Glass selection as "repetitive," "obnoxious," and "grating." They hypothesized that such different reactions would be captured in a measure of mood. The 65-question Profile of Mood States (POMS; Educational & Industrial Testing Service, 1971) was adapted for use in this experiment by drawing 3 questions from each of the six mood factors reported by the measure. The factors are Depression, Tension, Anger, Vigor, Fatigue, and Confusion. Two questions unrelated to the POMS were added, 1 to begin and 1 to end the measure, for a total of 20 questions on mood, all answered using a 5 point ordinal scale. Scholars predicted that the Glass selection would produce stronger indications of unpleasant mood relative to the Mozart sonata. Tapes for the Mozart and the Glass selections were prepared from the CD recordings and were played on a Sony CFD-545 unit. Rauscher *et al.* used the following experimental procedure. First, all subjects were administered 16 PF&C items as a pretest. On the basis of their performance, they were assigned to create three groups of "equivalent capabilities." The next day, the three groups were exposed to 10 min of a stimulus condition and immediately tested with 16 PF&C items. The stimulus conditions consisted of listening to either the Mozart or the Glass selection or sitting in silence. Each PF&C item was shown via an overhead projector for 1 min, with a 5-s warning of the end of that trial. The three groups repeated this daily procedure for 3 additional days, with the exception that the group that heard the Glass selection heard other material on succeeding days.

The procedure was slightly different. Because the 'Mozart effect' was significant only on the first post-treatment day in the study by Rauscher *et al.*, researchers restricted the experiment to the one post-treatment assessment. Performance on the PF&C pretest was not scored prior to group assignment. Instead, they assumed that random assignment would create equivalent groups. For schedule reasons, a time period of 48 hours elapsed between sessions for our participants.

Rauscher and Shaw's concern was that the pretest should not occur too close in time to the treatment condition; consequently, the lengthening of the interval by an additional 24 hours between pretest and treatment condition should not have affected the results adversely. Sessions were conducted in the early evening when the psychology building was quiet. Participants were recruited to create a group of 15 students per session; they arrived at the first session and were informed that they would be participating in a "puzzle experiment." The two sample PF&C items from the Stanford-Binet IQ measure were used to explain the task. The first sample item was projected onto a white screen measuring 3.5 m by 3.5 m. The experimenter explained the task using instructions slightly modified and abbreviated from the instructions provided by the Stanford-Binet measure. The second sample S-B PF&C item was then presented and explained.

After the participants were given the opportunity to ask questions, answer sheets were provided, and 16 PF&C items were projected for up to 1 min each (depending on how quickly all subjects had made their choice), with a 5 sec warning of the end of each 1-min period. The number of participants was limited to approximately 15 per session to ensure that distance from the screen and visibility of the projected PF&C item were equal for all participants. The second session began 48 hours later. Participants were reminded of the nature of the task, and answer sheets were distributed. Following exposure to the scheduled stimulus condition, participants were immediately tested on a new set of 16 PF&C items. The two sets of PF&C items were used in counterbalanced order across sessions and groups. After completing the PF&C task, the participants were immediately given the mood assessment instrument and instructed to indicate their mood when the PF&C task began. Performance on the PF&C items and answers to the mood questions were analyzed at a later date. The following table shows the results of the experiment:

MEAN NUMBER OF PF&C ITEMS ANSWERED CORRECTLY

		PRETEST		POST-TREATMENT	
LISTENING CONDITION	N	M	SE	M	SE
Mozart	44	9.66	0.56	11.77	0.48
Silence	42	9.88	0.47	11.60	0.43
Glass	39	9.90	0.70	12.15	0.62

The results are grouped according to subjects' assignment to treatment condition, but pretest results show performance on PF&C items prior to the treatment condition. The pretest results indicate that random assignment was successful in creating groups not significantly

23

different in initial task performance, $F(2, 122)$ = 0.05, p = .95. The post-treatment results, the mean number of PF&C items chosen correctly after exposure to the scheduled treatment condition, indicate that improvement in performance was approximately equal for all groups. This interpretation is supported by the results of analysis of variance: there was a significant main effect of session, $F(1, 122)$ = 76.1, $p < .001$, but no significant effect of treatment, $F(2, 122)$ = 0.11, p = .89, and no significant interaction of treatment by session, $F(2, 122)$ = 0.48, p = .62.

A more sensitive measure is to assess relative change at the level of the individual. An analysis of covariance was used to examine post-treatment performance, adjusted for an individual's initial performance on the PF&C task. There was no significant treatment effect observed with this procedure either, $F(2, 121)$ = 0.61, p = .55. Treatment condition did not influence cognitive task scores but did influence mood scores in the anticipated manner. Significant differences among the groups were seen for both the Tension factor, $F(2, 122)$ = 6.32, p = .002, and the Anger factor, $F(2, 122)$ = 7.21, p = .001. Tension scores were highest for the Glass group, intermediate for the silence group, and lowest for the Mozart group (Tukey HSD pair-wise probabilities: Glass vs. Mozart, p = .001; Glass vs. silence, p = .075).

Anger scores were also highest for the Glass group, intermediate for the silence group, and lowest for the Mozart group (Tukey HSD pair-wise probabilities: Glass vs. Mozart, p = .001; Glass vs. silence, p = .019).

An explanation for the results obtained after listening to music may lie in the manner in which music and spatial imaging are processed within the brain. There have been many studies on the localization of music perception. Techniques such as positron emission tomography (PET) and functional magnetic resonance scanning, together with studies on localized brain lesions, have shown that listening to music activates a wide distribution of brain areas. The primary auditory area lies classically in the transverse and superior temporal gyri, but particular components of musical appreciation involving rhythm, pitch, metre, melody, and timbre are processed in many different areas of the brain. These range from the prefrontal cortex and superior temporal gyrus to the precuneus of the parietal lobe, with much interconnection of the different networks activated. Rhythm and pitch discrimination are processed mainly in the left hemisphere whereas timbre and melody are found chiefly in the right. Appreciation of metre does not appear to show hemispheric preference.

Brain areas concerned with mental imaging as tested by spatial temporal tasks (such as the building of three-dimensional cube assemblies in sequence) were also mapped by PET scanning. The results show that the areas activated include the prefrontal, temporal and precuneus regions which overlap with those involved in music processing. It is suggested, therefore, that listening to music would prime the activation of those areas of the brain which are concerned with spatial reasoning.[2]

---

[2] A more impressive indication of a 'Mozart effect' is to be seen in epilepsy. The April 2001 edition of Journal of the Royal Society of Medicine assessed the possible health benefits of the music of Mozart. John Jenkins played Sonata K.448 to patients with epilepsy and found a decrease in epileptiform activity. In 23 of 29 patients with focal discharges or bursts of generalized spike and wave complexes who listened to the Mozart piano sonata K448 there was a significant decrease in epileptiform activity as shown by the EEG (electroencephalogram, brain wave activity). Some individual patients showed especially striking improvement. In one male, unconscious with status

Another explanation for increased test scores after listening to music would be the established theory of sensory stimulation. Stimulation excites the brain. It propagates more synapses between brain cells, ultimately creating more and more efficient conduits of brain function. Research indicates that there are "windows" of prime times for this activity.

---

epilepticus, ictal patterns were present 62% of the time, whereas during exposure to Mozart's music this value fell to 21%. In two other patients with status epilepticus continuous bilateral spike and wave complexes were recorded 90-100% of the time before the music, suddenly falling to about 50% 5 minutes after the music began. According to the British Epilepsy Organisation, research has suggested that apart from Mozart's K.448 and Piano Concerto No. 23 (K. 488), only one other piece of music has been found to have a similar effect; a song by the Greek composer Yanni, entitled "Acroyali/Standing in Motion" (version from Yanni Live at the Acropolis performed at the Acropolis). It was determined to have the 'Mozart effect', by the Journal of the Royal Society of Medicine because it was similar to Mozart's K.448 in tempo, structure, melodic and harmonic consonance and predictability.

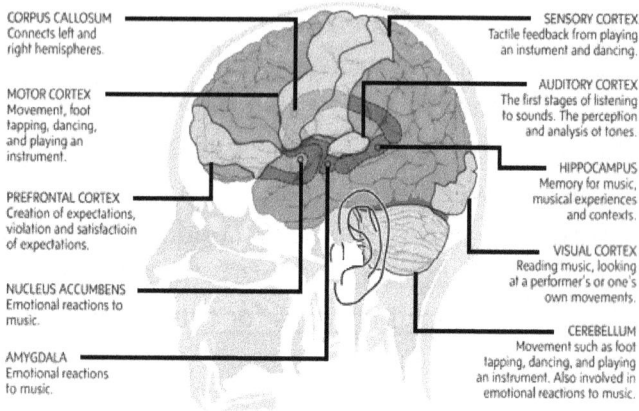

CORPUS CALLOSUM
Connects left and right hemispheres.

MOTOR CORTEX
Movement, foot tapping, dancing, and playing an instrument.

PREFRONTAL CORTEX
Creation of expectations, violation and satisfactioin of expectations.

NUCLEUS ACCUMBENS
Emotional reactions to music.

AMYGDALA
Emotional reactions to music.

SENSORY CORTEX
Tactile feedback from playing an instument and dancing.

AUDITORY CORTEX
The first stages of listening to sounds. The perception and analysis of tones.

HIPPOCAMPUS
Memory for music, musical experiences and contexts.

VISUAL CORTEX
Reading music, looking at a performer's or one's own movements.

CEREBELLUM
Movement such as foot tapping, dancing, and playing an instrument. Also involved in emotional reactions to music.

Most of the studies conducted so far demonstrate that much of this hard-wiring occurs prenatally and in early childhood. However, new studies are ever increasingly discovering that the brain can create new neural pathways long after childhood.

> We have this common internal neural language that we're born with and so if you can exploit that with the right stimuli then you're going to help the brain develop to do the things like reason.
> Dr. Gordon Shaw

When the brain is deprived of proper stimulation, it is believed that the neural pathways atrophy and ultimately are lost. Robert Dolman. M.D., founder of the National Academy for

Child Development, stated, "Sensory depriva-tion studies show us that sudden and nearly complete deprivation of stimulation through the five senses can lead to dramatic changes in the brain's efficiency with a partial loss of memory, a lowering of the I.Q., and personali-ty changes [...]". G. F. Reed, after analyzing studies of the cognitive effects of sensory dep-rivation, adds documentation. He found that subjects tested lower on most parts of tests of complex intellectual processes after periods of sensory deprivation, noting that "[...] logical, analytical thought, based on verbal symbols, deteriorates at the same time that there is more involuntary imagery in various sensory modalities, particularly the visual [...] stimulus deprivation appears to increase the kind of in-formation processing (such as) intuitive, con-figurational procedures at the expense of analysis, language, and logic."

The research stirred enough interest in the ac-ademic community to induce several other re-search teams to conduct similar experiments, with disparate results.

In 1994, Stough, Kerkin, Bates, and Mangan, at the University of Aukland, failed to produce any 'Mozart effect'. This may be due in part to the fact that the spatial IQ test used in New

Zealand was from Raven's Advanced Progressive Matrices, while the Rauscher *et al.* study used the Stanford-Binet Intelligence Scale. However, Kenealy and Monseth (1994) did use the same test (Stanford-Binet) to measure the 30 subjects they used in their study; these subjects showed no mean differences in scores after listening to Mozart, disco music, and silence.

In 1995, researchers (Newman, Rosenbach, Burns, Latimer, Matocha, and Vogt) at State University of New York at Albany replicated the original test. They broadened the test group to 114 subjects, and the age spread from 18 to 51 years with a mean age of 27.3. Not only did they find no similar increase in spatial IQ scores after listening to Mozart, but they also polled the subjects on previous musical background, and found no correlation to higher spatial IQ scores and music lessons earlier in life, or a correlation to higher spatial IQ scores and a preference for classical music.

Similar results were found the same year in a study by two Canadian University researchers, Nantais and Schellenberg. They reproduced the fundamental 'Mozart effect' experiment, and extended the study to investigate the relationship between listening to other forms of music and IQ. They found that the listener's preference to either music or the narration of a story, and not particularly listening to Mozart, made for improved test performance.

In 1996 and 1997, however, two studies at Ursinus College in Collegeville, Pennsylvania, by Rideout and Taylor supported and added further evidence to suggest a 'Mozart effect'. One study replicated the Rauscher *et al.* study and, using two different spatial-reasoning tasks, measured higher spatial IQ scores after listening to a Mozart selection. In the other study, Rideout and Laubach required 8 college students to listen to a Mozart piano sonata in one condition and no music in another condition. They measured changes in EEG prior to listening to the Mozart and then again after listening to the Mozart while engaged in two spatial-reasoning tasks. The EEG recordings were somewhat correlated with the students' performance, as increased brain activity was associated with an increase in spatial-reasoning performance after listening to the Mozart.

In 1998, Rideout, this time with Dougherty and Wernert, found that music with characteristics similar to the works of Mozart provided the same increase in temporary spatial IQ test scores.

Two other studies, both published in 1997, contradicted the 'Mozart effect'. Kenneth Steele, Ball, and Runk of Appalachian State University presented 36 college students a backwards digit span task, described as recalling 9-digit strings in reverse order, in three conditions – after listening to Mozart music, a recording of rain, or silence. The results found no difference between these three conditions. Carlson, Rama, Artchakov, and Linnankoski of the Institute of Biomedicine affiliated with University of Helsinki, Finland, chose monkeys to see if any 'Mozart effect' would show up in another animal. He used a memory task to test various experimental conditions including Mozart music, simple rhythms, white noise, and silence. The results were intriguing. The monkeys actually performed highest in the white noise condition and lowest in the Mozart music condition.

Perhaps inspired by the Carlson *et al.* test using monkeys, Rauscher and her colleagues chose to study the 'Mozart effect' on laboratory rats in 1998. These rats were exposed both in utero and for two months postpartum to Mozart's piano sonata. The other comparison groups included rats that were exposed in the same time frame to minimalist music, white noise, or silence. The rats that were exposed in the Mozart group learned to maneuver a T-maze considerably faster and with fewer errors than rats in the other three groups.

In 1998 Christopher Chabris, a graduate student at Harvard University (now a research fellow at Harvard Medical School and Massachusetts General Hospital), questioned the net result of studies on the 'Mozart effect' that had been done over the previous five years. In a pair of papers published together under the title *Prelude or Requiem for the 'Mozart Effect'?*, he reported a meta-analysis demonstrating that "any cognitive enhancement is small and does not reflect any change in IQ or reasoning ability in general, but instead derives entirely from performance on one specific type of cognitive task and has a simple neuropsychological explanation", called "enjoyment arousal". For example, he cites a study that found that "listening either to Mozart or to a passage from a Stephen King story enhanced subjects' performance in paper folding and cutting (one of the tests frequently employed by Rauscher and Shaw) but only for those who enjoyed what they heard". Steele *et al.* found that "listening to Mozart produced a 3-point increase relative to silence in one experiment and a 4-point decrease in the other experiment".[3]

In another study, the effect was replicated with the original Mozart music, but eliminated when the tempo was slowed down and major chords were replaced by minor chords.[4] His conclusion was that "There's nothing wrong with having young people listen to classical music, but it's not going to make them smarter".

Other skeptics have been convinced that a 'Mozart effect' does exist. Lois Hetland of the Harvard Graduate School of Education attempted to replicate earlier 'Mozart effect' studies in broader depth, including a total of 1014 subjects. Her findings were that the Mozart listening group outperformed other

[3] STEELE K. M., DALLA BELLA, S., PERETZ I., DUNLOP T., DAWE L. A., HUMPHREY G. K., SHANNON R. A., KIRBY JR. J. L. & OLMSTEAD C. G. (1999). *Prelude or requiem for the 'Mozart effect'?* NATURE, 400, 827.

[4] HUSAIN G., THOMPSON W.F. & SCHELLENBERG, E.G. (2002). *Effects of musical tempo and mode on arousal, mood, and spatial abilities: Re-examination of the "Mozart effect".* MUSIC PERCEPTION, 20, 151-171.

groups by a higher margin than could be explained by chance, although factors such as the subject's gender, musical tastes and training, innate spatial ability, and cultural background made a difference in the degree to which the Mozart would increase test scores. She did not find the 'Mozart effect' to be as strong as Rauscher *et al.* had found, however. Her belief is that even these small effects are impressive because so many other factors could obscure them. "In the early stages of research in a field, we would expect the measured effect to be small until we learn to separate the signal from the noise in the research method." She noted that Chabris had only studied the experiments that compared listening to Mozart to silence, and which had not included listening to other compositions.

Psychologist Eric Seigel at Elmhurst College, Illinois, (who had been a self-described skeptic), set out to disprove the 'Mozart effect'. He chose a different spatial reasoning test, one that involves the subject's ability to discriminate between shifted positions of the letter E as various rotations are given. The brief time that it takes to judge whether the letter is the same or different effectively measures spatial reasoning. Subjects in the Mozart listening group did significantly better. "It was as though they had practiced the test [...] we have another way to measure the Mozart Effect", says Seigel.

Rauscher and Shaw explained the inconsistent results of the 'Mozart effect' tests in a work published in Perception and Motor Skills (1998), Vol. 86, pp. 835-841. They stated that the reason the results do not concur is that the various studies designed to find the 'Mozart effect' have utilized diverse subjects and different methodological designs, such as music compositions, listening conditions, and measures. They announced in fact that they had scientific proof that piano and singing instruction are superior to computer instruction in enhancing patients' abstract reasoning skills.[5]

The experiment included three groups of preschoolers: one group received private piano/keyboard lessons and singing lessons; a second group received private computer lessons; and a third group received no training.

---

[5] These theories are controversial. The relationship of sound and music (both played and listened to) for cognitive function and various physiological metrics has been explored in studies with no definitive results.

Those children who received piano/keyboard training performed 34% higher on tests measuring spatial- temporal ability than the others. These findings indicate that music uniquely enhances higher brain functions required for mathematics, chess, science and engineering (Neurological Research, February 1997).

Shaw and Rauscher have stimulated an industry. They have also created their own institute: The Music Intelligence Neural Development Institute (M.I.N.D.). There is so much research going on to prove the wondrous effects of music that a website has been created just to keep track of all the new developments: MUSICA, which has a section just on the 'Mozart effect'.

Shaw and Rauscher claim that their work has been misrepresented. What they have shown is "that there are patterns of neurons that fire in sequences, and that there appear to be pre-existing sites in the brain that respond to specific frequencies." This is not quite the same as showing that listening to Mozart increases intelligence in children. Nevertheless, Shaw is not going to wait for the hard evidence to pour in before he cashes in on the desire of parents to enhance their children's intelligence. He has a book and a CD out called

Keeping Mozart in Mind. He and his colleagues are convinced that since spatio-temporal reasoning is essential for many higher order cognitive tasks, stimulating the area of the brain associated with spatio-temporal reasoning and doing spatio-temporal exercises will increase a person's intelligence for math, engineering, chess, and science. They even have a software program for sale, which uses no language and aims at exercising spatio-temporal skills with the help of an animated penguin.

Shaw and Rauscher may have spawned an industry, but the mass media and others have created a kind of alternative science that supports the industry. Exaggerated and false claims about music have become so commonplace that it is probably a waste of time to try to correct them. For example, Jamal Munshi, an associate professor of Business Administration at Sonoma State University, collects tidbits of misinformation and gullibility. He used to post them on the Internet as "Weird but True," including the claim that Shaw and Rauscher showed that listening to Mozart's sonata for two pianos in D major "increased SAT[6] scores of students by 51 points." Actual-

---

[6] The SAT, or the Reasoning Test (formerly Scholastic Aptitude Test and Scholastic Assess-

ly, Shaw and Rauscher gave 36 UC Irvine students a paper folding and cutting test and found the Mozart group showed a temporary 8-9 point increase over their scores when they took the test after either a period of silence or listening to a relaxation tape. (Munshi also claims that science cannot explain how a fly flies. Scientists have been working hard on this crucial problem, so we should give them their due. Some even claim to know how insects fly).

A former musician and music writer, Don Campbell was one of the first people who saw the commercial opportunities in this new phenomena. His 1997 book, entitled *The Mozart Effect: Tapping the Power of Music to Heal the Body, Strengthen the Mind, and Unlock the Creative Spirit*", began to exploit the situation. He released collections of Mozart's music packaged as learning aides for children and adults alike. He trademarked the term 'The Mozart Effect' for his growing line of commercial products. His collection now includes 18 books on the subject and 16 different albums of Mozart's music. He has taken the concept to much greater lengths, no longer claiming

---

ment Test) is a college admissions test in the United States.

that Mozart's music just increases intelligence. He says it also helps with healing, emotions and creativity and does not let the fact that there is no scientific basis for his claims get in his way. One of his recent books, *Mozart Effect for Children*, claims that Mozart's music enhances "deep rest and rejuvenation", "intelligence and learning", and "creativity and imagination". He defines the term as "an inclusive term signifying the transformational powers of music in health, education, and well-being. It represents the general use of music to reduce stress, depression, or anxiety; induce relaxation or sleep; activate the body; and improve memory or awareness. Innovative and experimental uses of music and sound can improve listening disorders, dyslexia, attention deficit disorder, autism, and other mental and physical disorders and diseases". His Mozart compilation collection even includes a version of *Don Giovanni* for the fetus (Dowd, 2007). By the end of the 20th century it was common knowledge among mothers and educators that listening to classical music, especially Mozart, was a must to help aid in the cognitive development of their children.

Don Campbell, however, has exaggerated and distorted the work of Shaw, Rauscher, and others for his own benefit. He has trade-marked the expression 'The Mozart Effect' and peddles himself and his products at *www.mozarteffect.com*. Campbell claims that he made a blood clot in his brain disappear by humming, praying, and envisioning a vibrating hand on the right side of his skull. Uncritical supporters of alternative medicine don't question this claim, though it is one of those safe claims that can't be proved or disproved. He might as well claim that angels took the clot away. (One wonders why, if music is so good for you, he got a blood clot in the first place. Accidentally listening to rap music?)

The claims that Campbell makes for music are of an almost rococo flamboyance. And like the rococo, just about as substantive (Campbell claims music can cure just about anything that ails you). His evidence is usually anecdotal; even this he misinterprets. Some things he gets completely wrong.

And the whole structure of his argument collapses under simple common sense. If Mozart's music were able to improve health, why was Mozart himself so frequently sick? If listening to Mozart's music increases intelligence and encourages spirituality, why aren't the world's smartest and most spiritual people Mozart specialists?

The lack of evidence for the 'Mozart effect' has not deterred Campbell from becoming a favorite on the lecture circuit with the naive and uncritical.

When McCall's wants advice on how to lose the blues with music, when PBS wants to interview an expert on how the voice can energize you, when IBM wants a consultant to use music to increase efficiency and harmony in the workplace, when the National Association of Cancer Survivors wants a speaker on the healing powers of music, they turn to Campbell.

That said, it is not surprising that the governors of Tennessee and Georgia started programs that give a Mozart CD to every newborn. Florida's legislature passed a law requiring that classical music be played daily in state-funded childcare and educational programs. Hundreds of hospitals were given free CDs of classical music in May of 1999 by the National Academy of Recording Arts and Sciences Foundation. These are well-intentioned gestures, but are they based on solid research that classical music increases a child's intelligence or an adult's healing process? And isn't it likely that the money could be better spent? Yes, according to Kenneth Steele, a psychology professor at Appalachian State University, and John Bruer, head of the James S. McDonnell Foundation in St. Louis. Contrary to all the hype, they claim that there is no real intelligence enhancing or health benefit to listening to Mozart. Steele and his colleagues, Karen Bass and Melissa Crook, claim that they followed the protocols set forth by Shaw and Rauscher but could not "find any kind of effect at all," even though their study tested 125 students. They concluded that "there is little evidence to support intervention programs based on the existence of the Mozart effect". Their research appears in the July 1999 issue of Psychological Science. Two years later, several researchers reported in the same journal that when an effect is observed after intervention with music it is due to "a boost in mood and arousal" (Willingham 2006).

While some supportive reports have been published,[7] studies with positive results have

---

[7] WILSON T., BROWN T. (1997). *Reexamination of the effect of Mozart's music on spatial task performance. Journal of Psychology*. 131 (4), 365. Re-

tended to be associated with any form of music that has energetic and positive emotional qualities.[8] Among children, some studies suggest no effect on IQ or spatial ability;[9] whereas others suggest that the effect can be elicited with energetic popular music that the children enjoy.[10] The weight of subsequent evidence supports either a null effect, or short-term effects related to increases in mood and arousal, with mixed results published after the initial report in *Nature*.[11]

---

trieved December 4, 2007, from EbscoHost Research Databases.

[8] THOMPSON W.F., SCHELLENBERG E.G. & HUSAIN G. (2001). *Mood, arousal, and the Mozart effect*. PSYCHOLOGICAL SCIENCE, 12(3), 248-251.

[9] MCKELVIE P., JASON LOW J. (2002). *Listening to Mozart does not improve children's spatial ability: Final curtains for the Mozart effect*. BRITISH JOURNAL OF DEVELOPMENTAL PSYCHOLOGY, 20, 241–258.

[10] SCHELLENBERG E.G., & HALLAM S. (2005). *Music listening and cognitive abilities in 10 and 11 year olds: The Blur effect*. ANNALS OF THE NEW YORK ACADEMY OF SCIENCES, 1060, 202-209.

[11] BRIDGETT D.J., CUEVAS J. (2000), *Effects of listening to Mozart and Bach on the performance of a mathematical test*, PERCEPTUAL AND MOTOR SKILLS, 90. pp. 1171–1175.

Government bodies also became involved in analyzing the wealth (some 300+ articles as of 2005) of reports. A German report concluded, for instance, that "... passively listening to Mozart — or indeed any other music you enjoy — does not make you smarter. But more studies should be done to find out whether music lessons could raise your child's IQ in the long term".[12]

Popular presentations of the 'Mozart effect', including Alex Ross's comment that "listening to Mozart actually makes you smarter" and Zell Miller's "don't you feel smarter" query to the Georgia legislature, almost always tie it to "intelligence." Rauscher, one of the original researchers, has disclaimed this idea. In a 1999 reply to an article challenging the effect,[13] published along with the article, she wrote (emphasis added):

---

[12] ABBOTT ALISON, *Mozart doesn't make you clever*, CF. www.nature.com/news/2007/00409/full/news070409-13.html.

[13] STEELE K. M., DALLA BELLA, S., PERETZ I., DUNLOP T., DAWE L. A., HUMPHREY G. K., SHANNON R. A., KIRBY JR. J. L. & OLMSTEAD C. G. (1999). *Prelude or requiem for the 'Mozart effect'?, op.cit.*.

Our results on the effects of listening to Mozart's Sonata for Two Pianos in D Major K. 448 on spatial–temporal task performance have generated much interest but several misconceptions, many of which are reflected in attempts to replicate the research. The comments by Chabris and Steele et al. echo the most common of these: that listening to Mozart enhances intelligence. We made no such claim. The effect is limited to spatial–temporal tasks involving mental imagery and temporal ordering.

On efforts like Miller's budget proposal, and the press attention surrounding the effect, Rauscher has said, "I don't think it can hurt. I'm all for exposing children to wonderful cultural experiences. But I do think the money could be better spent on music education programs".[14]

While it is clear that exposure to Mozart does not raise IQ, studies of the effects of music have explored as diverse areas as its links to

---

[14] GOODE ERICA, *Mozart For Baby? Some Say, Maybe Not*, THE NEW YORK TIMES, 1999-08-03 p. f1: Rauscher, "the money could be better spent on music education programs".

seizure onset[15] or research in animals suggesting that even exposure in-utero in rats improves their maze learning. [16] The original claim continues to influence public life. For instance a German sewage treatment plant plays Mozart music to break down the waste faster, reports the UK Guardian. Anton Stucki, chief operator of the Treuenbrietzen plant was quoted as saying, "We think the secret is in the vibrations of the music, which penetrate everything — including the water, the sewage and the cells".[17]

In his book, *The Myth of the First Three Years*, Bruer attacks not only the 'Mozart effect' but several other related myths based on the misinterpretation of recent brain research.

---

[15] HUGHES J., DAABOUL Y., FINO J., SHAW G. (1998). *The Mozart effect on epileptiform activity*, Clin Electroencephalogr, 29 (3), 109-19. Retrieved December 3, 2007, from Pubmed Database.

[16] *Improved maze learning through early music exposure in rats*. Neurol. Res. (National Center for Biotechnology Information) 20 (5): 427–32. July 1998.

[17] CONNOLLY KATE (2 June 2010), *Sewage plant plays Mozart to stimulate microbes*, The Guardian, Retrieved 8 April 2011.

The 'Mozart effect' is an example of how science and the media mix in our world. A suggestion in a few paragraphs in a scientific journal becomes a universal truth in a matter of months, eventually believed even by the scientists who initially recognized how their work had been distorted and exaggerated by the media. Others, smelling the money, jump on the bandwagon and play to the crowd, adding their own myths, questionable claims, and distortions to the mix. In this case, many uncritical supporters line up to defend the faith because at stake here is the future of our children. We then have books, tapes, CDs, institutes, government programs, etc. Soon the myth is believed by millions as a scientific fact. In this case, the process met with little critical resistance because we already know that music can affect feelings and moods, so why shouldn't it affect intelligence and health, even if only slightly and temporarily? It's just commonsense, right? Yes; and all the more reason to be skeptical.

The popular excitement about the 'Mozart effect' is due to its claim to be a brief, easy remedy to improve intellectual skills. However, previous attempts to increase IQ scores demonstrate how difficult it is to produce even a small, short-lived gain (Spitz, 1986). Considering the duration and depth of many intervention programs, an effect from short periods of listening to music does not seem feasible in principle. The results of this experiment, and experiments in other laboratories, are consistent with such an expectation.

In a nutshell, there is little evidence to support basing intellectual enhancement programs on the existence of the causal relationship termed the 'Mozart effect'.

MOZART AND FREEMASONRY

The mysterious fraternal organization known as Freemasonry can trace its origins all the way back to the Middle Ages.[18] But its

---

[18] 'Freemason' is an Anglicization of the Khemetic words PHREE and MESSEN, meaning 'Children of Light', 'Reborn children'. The concept of 'rebirth' implied in 'mes' is the same 'mas' found in holding a 'mass' or in Christ-'mas', in 'Mos'-es. It corresponds to the sun/son that is reborn at the winter solstice (Dec 25th), worldwide known as "Christ-mas". Egyptian "Mas/mes" also means to pour/ anoint, and this refers to renewal within the human body (as without, so within), same as the Sanskrit "kri", as in "Kri"shna. Heru's most ancient name was "Chresh Mes", the sun born at Christmas, then re-born again after 9 months as spiritual seed in Virgo (the "virgin"). A "phre mes" is therefore a Heru, or Horus, or Krishna, or Christ. A "Ma-son" is also a "widow's son", because Heru`s father was "killed" by Seth before his birth (the sun- set, which takes place in Virgo, the virgin, ruled by Mercury, this is why "Satan" has little horns). The son/sun as the "redeemer", is the spiritual "son of man", which is Aquarius, the human being within the animal circle (Zodiac), who pours out his waters (origin of "baptizing"). It is also Ma-son as in Ma`at- Ra, the justice/love of
50

roots took hold sometime at the end of the 16th century with the organization of the first Masonic lodges, basic structures described as a meeting of a group of Masons. It was not until the early 18th century that Freemasonry was reorganized into larger more distinct units whose presence spread across Europe.

The oldest document that makes reference to Masons is the *Regius Poem*, printed about 1390, which was a copy of an earlier work. The work was published in 1840 by Mr. James Orchard Halliwell, under the title of *A poem of the Constitutions of Masonry* from the original manuscript in the King's Library of the British Museum.

Mr. Halliwell, who afterwards adopted the name of Phillips, says that the manuscript

---

the energy contained in the rays of the sun ("Ra" does not mean "sun", the word for sun is Aton). Every human being is a "Ma-son" by birthright! Even the single letters of the word 'Mason' carry a meaning: **M**em (mother), **A**leph (father), **S**in (fell short, "ate fruit"), **A**yin (all-seeing eye), **N**un (fish, seed, first born). It is a tiny leftover from the times, when symbols were regarded higher than letters and right brain thinking was still the main way of operating, as communication through visual imagery is superior to left brain "reading".

formerly belonged to Charles Theyer, a well-known collector of the 17th century. The manuscript is rhymed in verse, and consists of 794 lines.

In 1717, four lodges in London formed the first Grand Lodge of England, and records from that point on are more complete. Within 30 years, the fraternity had spread throughout Europe and the American Colonies. George Washington was a Mason, Benjamin Franklin served as the head of the fraternity in Pennsylvania, as did Paul Revere and Joseph Warren in Massachusetts. Other well-known Masons involved with the founding of America included John Hancock, John Sullivan, Lafayette, Baron Fredrick von Stuben, Nathanael Greene, and John Paul Jones. Another Mason, Chief Justice John Marshall, shaped the Supreme Court into its present form.

During the late 1700s it was one of the organizations most responsible for spreading the ideals of the Enlightenment: the dignity of man and the liberty of the individual, the right of all persons to worship as they choose, the formation of democratic governments, and the importance of public education. In other words, Freemasonry began a new and worrying thing to many in power: its stated principles of humanism and equality made it seem revolutionary to the nobility and the Church, and it was widely believed after the shocking events of 1789 that the Freemasons (in particular the Illuminati with whom Mozart was most closely linked) had initiated the French Revolution. Although, of itself, not a political force, it attracted the attention of many who did have political power, and thus became a danger to the established order. Based largely on ideas of what Egyptian and Eleusinian ritual were all about, Freemasonry also encapsulated the secrecy of an underground religious order, and an affinity with Nature.

Masons believed that by regressing to a state of primitive humanity (Rousseau's 'noble savage') men could become equal parts of society once more. The vast disparity between the wealth of the noble minority and the poverty of the illiterate majority was seen as the greatest evil of Mankind, and it was to this end that the Masons worked to establish communes and a sense of equality and fraternity.

During the 1800s and early 1900s, Freemasonry grew dramatically. At that time, the government had provided no social "safety net," and the Masonic tradition of founding orphanages, homes for widows, and homes for the aged provided the only security many people knew.

As a pianist, little Wolfgang had been an infant prodigy, exhibited by his father throughout Europe; in Vienna he was a recognized and admired composer. The very year of his initiation his first great opera, *Le nozze di Figaro*, had been produced in Paris. This was, however, before the days of copyright law and the earnings of genius were meager. During the 18th century, Freemasonry in Vienna had a political as well as a benevolent side. It counted as its members many highly placed politicians and ecclesiastics whose ideal was the regeneration of humanity by moral means. It was hated by the Catholic Church and certain despotic political authorities who deemed it dangerous, both to religion and the well-being of the state. The Church, however, even as today in certain Latin countries, did not consider it expedient to challenge high-placed persons nominally its members but also of the Fraternity. The Empress Maria Theresa had been one who was opposed to Masonry and, in 1743, had ordered a Viennese Lodge raided, forcing its Master and her husband, Francis I, to make his escape by a secret staircase. The

Emperor Joseph II (1780-90) was favorably in-clined to the Fraternity, although the clergy did their best to get the Lodges suppressed.

Such was the Masonic milieu when Wolfgang Mozart became a Master Mason. He must have been greatly moved and inspired by his experience. Almost immediately he composed his Freemason's Funeral Music and his music for the opening and closing of a Lodge. He now composed his opera, *Don Giovanni*, and his three great symphonies – the E flat, the G minor and the C major, as well as a great number of concertos and chamber-music works.

Mozart was admitted as an apprentice to the Viennese Masonic lodge called *Zur Wohl-tätigkeit* (Beneficence) on 14 December 1784 and spent a total of seven years as a Mason. He was promoted to journeyman Mason on 7 January 1785, and became a master Mason "shortly thereafter". Mozart also attended the meetings of another lodge, called *Zur wahren Eintracht* (True Concord). According to Otto Erich Deutsch, this lodge was "the largest and most aristocratic in Vienna. Mozart, as the best of the musical 'Brothers', was welcome in all the lodges"; it was headed by the naturalist Ignaz von Born.

Mozart's own lodge *Zur Wohltätigkeit* was consolidated with two others in December of 1785, under the Imperial reform of Masonry (the *Freimaurerpatent*, "Masonic Decree") of 11 December 1785, and thus Mozart came to belong to the lodge called *Zur Neugekrönten Hoffnung* (New Crowned Hope).

At least as far as surviving Masonic documents can prove, Mozart was well regarded by his fellow Masons. Many of his friends were Masons!

During his visit to Vienna in 1785, Mozart's father Leopold also became a Mason. Mozart's position within the Masonic movement, according to Maynard Solomon, lay with the rationalist, Enlightenment-inspired membership, as opposed to those members oriented toward mysticism and the occult.[19] This rationalist faction is identified by Katherine Thomson as the Illuminati, a masonically inspired group which was founded by Bavarian professor of canon law Adam Weishaupt, who was also a friend of Mozart. The Illuminati espoused the Enlightenment-inspired, humanist views proposed by the French philosophers Jean-Jacques Rousseau and Denis Diderot. For ex-

---

[19] SOLOMON MAYNARD, *Mozart: A Life*, Hammersmith: Harper Collins, 1995, p. 327.

ample, the Illuminati contended that social rank was not coincident with nobility of the spirit, but that people of lowly class could be noble in spirit just as nobly born could be mean-spirited.

This view appears in Mozart's operas; for example, in *Le nozze di Figaro*, an opera based on a play by Pierre Beaumarchais – another Freemason, the lowly-born Figaro is the hero and the Count Almaviva is the boor. However, Masonic scholars themselves, and non-Masonic scholars who have studied the matter more closely strongly dispute both the conflation of Freemasonry with Illuminati elements per se, and especially Mozart as Mason in relation to these elements.

The Freemasons used music in their ceremonies, and adopted Rousseau's humanist views on the meaning of music. "The purpose of music in the [Masonic] ceremonies is to spread good thoughts and unity among the members" so that they may be "united in the idea of innocence and joy"; music should "inculcate feelings of humanity, wisdom and patience, virtue and honesty, loyalty to friends, and finally an understanding of freedom".

These views suggest a musical style quite unlike the style of the Galant, fashionable from the 1720s to the 1770s. Galant style music was typically melodic with harmonic accompaniment, rather than polyphonic; and the melodic line was often richly ornamented with trills, runs and other virtuosic effects. The style promoted by the Masonic view was much less virtuosic and unornamented. Mozart's style of composition is often referred to as "humanist" and is in accord with this Masonic view of music.

Through his close association with the Masonic and Illuminati movements, Mozart was seen as a dangerous political figure, determined to give away the secrets of the Masonic truths he believed in through his music. It is just as plausible that the enemies of the Masons, or a rival group of Masons who believed in the absolute sacred secrecy of their order, could have sought to destroy the young composer. Did Mozart betray Masonic secrets in his work? He certainly showed strong influence from the Masons, even before his official inauguration into the Brotherhood in 1785 and his music is littered with devices which suggest Masonic ideals and beliefs.

At various points during Mozart's life, the authorities clamped down on Masonry, making it illegal and heretical to be a part of a Lodge or to possess tomes of Masonic thought. This lack of acceptance in mainstream society of Masonic beliefs led to Mozart's widow, Constanze, destroying many of his books and papers in case they could be used to blacken his name posthumously and thus bring shame upon their children. It was undoubtedly Mozart's stubbornness to renounce his humanism which in later years cost him his popularity and his status with the crowned heads of Europe, whilst establishing him as a friend of the common people. He stood on the threshold of a new era, when composers and musicians would no longer be viewed as mere servants, but as artisans and craftsmen in their own right. His tragedy was that whilst he saw this coming, he was too radical and ahead of his own time to take advantage of it in the way subsequent businessmen/composers were to; only decades after his death.

That Mozart passionately believed in the ideals of Freemasonry is evident from much of his work, in which cantatas and concertos written specifically for Masonic friends, Lodges and events figure too highly to be ignored. He was not simply just a Mason, however. Related to this – and perhaps because of it – he had a profound attitude to death, especially his own death. He was often ill – with small-pox as a child, and with fevers and depression as an adult – and on several occasions he was close enough to death to gain a morbid fascination with it. However, he never feared dying. In a letter to his father he confessed that:

> Death... is the true goal of our existence. I have formed... such close relations with this best and truest friend of mankind, that his image is not only no longer terrifying to me, but is indeed very soothing and consoling! And I thank my God for graciously granting me the opportunity [...] of learning that death is the key which unlocks the door to our true happiness. I never lie down at night without reflecting that – young as I am – I may not live to see another day.

This idea of death as the key to the door of happiness (illumination or wisdom) is a Masonic one, and clearly something very close to Mozart's heart. When he was finally dying, it was with great difficulty that a priest could be found who was willing to administer the last rites to him. His unorthodox views, and his close association with the Illuminati, condemned him in the eyes of the priesthood, despite there being no actual hypocrisy in being both a good Mason and a good Christian.

Mozart's blackest period seems to have begun in 1788. He was heavily in debt, assailed by 'black thoughts', his wife Constanze was away recuperating from a fever, and Mozart himself was ill. However, he was also highly productive at this time. He wrote three symphonies in six weeks, expressing his deepest fears, his struggles against the darkness, and his renewed hope in the future of humanity.

Despite his vast opus of compositions, Mozart was frequently too poor to live comfortably, but he refused to compromise his work for the sake of money. When his publisher, Hoffmeister, suggested to write more popularly, he retorted that if he could not write what he chose – instead of what the public wanted and would pay for – he would 'write nothing more, and go hungry, or may the devil take me!'. The worst efforts of the censors to ban or decimate his works he bore with outspoken anger, and he scorned the audience who did not appreciate his music as 'mere brute beasts'.

The infamous *Requiem* – left unfinished at Mozart's death and completed by his pupil Süssmayr – has been the subject of controversy and speculation for more than 200 years. It had been commissioned by a German Count in memory of his wife, but since he apparently intended to pass it off as his own work, he sent his agent to Mozart without revealing his identity. Mozart, who was already ill, became obsessed with the idea that he was writing his own requiem. He started to work on it but set it aside to complete *Die Zauberflöte* and *La Clemenza di Tito*, which had been commissioned for the coronation of the Bohemian King Leopold II in September 1791. The exhausting schedule of composition, on top of his poverty and ill health, meant that the Requiem was never completed by Mozart. Although the idea that he was composing it for his own death seems to have been merely an aberration of his own personal madness, it remains the most evocative tribute to his life, his work and his genius.

The worldwide fraternal organization of Freemasonry calls itself "a beautiful system of morality veiled in allegory and illustrated by symbols." It is in fact nothing more than an educational society, attempting to teach its members a moral philosophy of life – it strives for a regeneration of humanity by moral means. But the secrecy of this the world's largest brotherhood, deemed necessary to ensure that aspiring members truly meet their moral standards, has always evoked a vague feeling of unease and suspicion. And this was even more so the case during the revolutionary age of the late 18th century.

During this time, Freemasonry also had a pronounced political aspect to it. After all, the era of Enlightenment brought with it The American and French Revolutions and the old monarchies of Europe were nervous about anything suggesting social reform or change. Hadn't the revolt of the American colonies been led by many a Mason; George Washington, Thomas Jefferson and Benjamin Franklin among them? Hadn't the Masons in France been behind the push for republican government?

Before the Revolution, Austrian emperors, for instance, often took a benign view of Masonry's belief that man is perfectible through reason. But in this revolutionary context they too suspected treason when the Masons argued that there would be no need for monarchs in a fully enlightened society. And into this turbulent period enters a harmless musician, "Brother Mozart".

Mozart's masonic music falls into three broad categories: music he wrote specifically for the lodge, music intended for the public but conceived on masonic themes, and music he wrote for other purposes, but which was adapted – either by himself or others – for masonic use:[20]

- ✓ K.53 Lied: *An die Freude*. Masonic poem set to music;
- ✓ K.93 Psalm 129: *De Profundis Clamavi* for mixed choir and orchestra. Composed in Salzburg in 1771 and later adapted to masonic use by the composer;
- ✓ K.148 *O Heiliges Band* (The hallowed bond of friendship) for tenor and piano. Composed in 1772 and adopted for Freemasonry; probably sung at refreshment;
- ✓ K.273 *Graduale ad Festum B.M.V.: "Sancta Maria, mater Dei"* for mixed choir and orchestra. Composed in 1777 and later adopted by the lodge;
- ✓ K. 345 *Thamos, Thamos Konig in Agypten*. Drama by Tobias Philipp Baron von Gebler (1773, revised 1779). Mozart's incidental music themes are claimed to be heavily masonic;

---

[20] The list was compiled in part by Charles Tupper, cited in Mozart and his masonic music Robert G. Davis, Philalethes Society (12/06/2006).

- ✓ K.410 *Canonic Adagio* for 2 basset horns and bassoon. Composed in 1784, ritual procession music;
- ✓ K.411 *Adagio* for 2 clarinets and 3 basset horns. Probably intended as a processional entrance for the lodge;
- ✓ K.429 Cantata: *Dir, Seele des Weltalls*. Composed for a public masonic celebration;
- ✓ K.468 *Gesellenreise*. (Fellow Craft's Journey) Bro. Franz Joseph v. Ratschky's verse on the journey to greater knowledge, first performed in Lodge True Concord on 16 April 1785 for Mozart's father's Fellowcraft Degree;
- ✓ K.471 Cantata: *Die Maurerfreude* (Masonic Joy). Words by Franz Petran, composed on 20 April 1785 and first performed in Lodge Zur gerkronten Hoffnung (Lodge Crowned Hope) on 24 April 1785 to honor Ignaz von Born, Grand Master of the United Lodges;
- ✓ K.477 *Maurerische Trauermusik* (Masonic Funeral Music). Composed in Vienna on 10 November 1785 for a Lodge of Sorrows held by Lodge Crowned Hope a week later for the funerals of Bro. Georg August, Duke of Mecklenburg-Streletz and Bro. Franz, Count Esterhazy of Galantha;
- ✓ K.482 *Piano Concerto in Eb Major*. Written for and performed at a concert given by

the Lodge Zur gekronten Hoffnung, 15 December 1785;

- ✓ K.483 *Zerfließet heut', geliebte Brüder*. Composed in December of 1785 for Lodge Crowned Hope. Text by Bro. Augustin Veith Edler von Schittlersberg, Senior Warden of Lodge True Concord for the opening of a lodge;
- ✓ K.484 *Ihr unsre neuen Leiter*. Composed in December of 1785 for Lodge Crowned Hope. Text by Bro. Augustin Veith Edler von Schittlersberg, Senior Warden of Lodge True Concord for the opening of a lodge;
- ✓ K.543 *Symphony No. 39 in Eb*. Written as a celebration of the Craft and the joy of living;
- ✓ K.546 *Adagio and Fugue in C Minor*. Not originally written for masonic use;
- ✓ K.617 *Adagio and Rondo* for Flute, Oboe, Viola, Cello, and Celesta. Written while Mozart was working on *Die Zauberflöte* and performed at refreshment in lodge;
- ✓ K.618 *Motet: Ave Verum Corpus*. Not originally written for masonic use;
- ✓ K.619 Cantata: *Die ihr des unermeßlichen Weltalls Schöpfer ehrt*. Text by Franz Zeigenhagen, composed at the request of his lodge;
- ✓ K.623 *Eine Kleine Freimaurerkantate* (Little Masonic Cantata). Composed in Vienna on

15 November 1791 with the text purport-edly by Bro. Emanuel Schikaneder. Written for the dedication of Lodge Zur neugekronten Hoffnung (Lodge New Crowned Hope). Performance held 18 November 1791. This was the last work completed by Mozart;

- ✓ K.623b Chorus: *Lasst uns mit geschlungen Handen*. Written as part of the same dedication service as above;
- ✓ K.626 *Requiem Mass*. Later adopted for masonic funerals;
- ✓ According to lodge records, Mozart wrote the music for two additional songs during 1785 — *Des Todes Werk and Vollbracht ist die Arbeit der Meister* (The Work of Death and The Work of the Masters is Finished)— which have been lost.

But it was Mozart's last opera, *Die Zauberflöte*, which is said to offer the most esoteric, Masonic symbolism and meaning. Several years before its appearance, Lorenzo Da Ponte had assisted the librettist Mazzola with the Masonic opera Osiris, written by Johann Gottlieb Naumann. The opera has some traceable similarities to *Die Zauberflöte*, if not musical, then Masonical. Test scenes for Osiris used Egypt as its setting, and the struggle between good and evil was at the forefront of the libretto itself.

Although it is accepted that Schikaneder wrote the libretto for Mozart's opera, there has been some dispute about *Die Zauberflöte*'s authorship. Schikaneder's wayward career and lack of any long-standing membership in any Masonic lodge may have fueled the suspect tales of false-authorship. In 1849, rumors were rife that Johann Georg Metzler (known as Giesecke) may have been responsible for the actual libretto. Julius Cornet, a tenor and opera director, published Die Oper in Deutschland und das Theater der Neuzeit (1849), which stated that Giesecke wrote the libretto and probably desired to remain anonymous for political reasons. The information was supplied to Cornet by Giesecke himself, so it is largely circumstantial and doesn't seem to warrant any further support.

Schikaneder's standing within Free-Masonry was altogether haphazard to say the least; research done by Brother Dr. Bernhard Beuer of Bayreuth traces Schikaneder's life as a Mason. Beuer's work states that Schikaneder entered "the craft" for worldly reasons, and was certainly not above anything scandalous or unethical, providing it was profitable.

Schikaneder's letters petitioning admission to the Masons shows his need for membership in a vagrant way:

> Deeply revered gentlemen, Not curiosity or selfishness but the most sincere esteem of your exalted assembly motivates by most humble prayer for admission to your sanctuary from which, in spite of the greatest secrecy, radiates a glimmer of nobility, humanity and wisdom. Enlighten me by your wise teachings, make me in your image, and I will remain with warmest thanks,
> Your most honoring and humble servant,
> Johann Emanuel Schikaneder

Schikaneder's letter is revealing, and shows his need for acceptance to a formal organization. The short letter also highlights his ability to stress (or at least react to) the dramatic element and self-promotion; certainly two character traits found in his Papageno.

One of the more intriguing elements of *Die Zauberflöte* is its roots in the Singspiel tradition on the one hand, and the opera's ability to move itself outside of that same tradition on the other. Indeed, the opera has never left the active repertoire, and perhaps the proper blend of thematic, formal and musical elements could serve as testimony to its long-standing success.

"Singspiel" as a formal approach to opera-theater has long been associated with the German language. "Singspiel" as a word however, has been loosely translated. Singspiel is generally accepted as the German equivalent to the French Opéra Comique. Ironically, Opéra Comique has been invariably linked to the French, yet both Singspiel and Opéra Comique take their cues from the Italian roots of Opera Buffa.

Singspiel was one of the reactions against opera seria and opera buffa, but for different reasons: opera seria had all but died by the end of the 18th century. The opera seria audience was ever-smaller, and the patricians seemed to be the only ones interested in the stationary nature of the stories. Opera buffa suffered a similar fate, yet it was for quite the opposite reason. Italian opera buffa became a revolving door of deceived lovers and cowardly dilettantes. The critics are suspicious — they've seen the show before.

Singspiel was, in *Die Zauberflöte*'s case, to be equated more with the Opéra Comique tradition. Mozart's reference of the Opéra Comique tradition combined with the Lyric

Theater could be traced to Jean-Jacques Rousseau's *Le Devin du village*. The work dates from 1752 and sets a prototype within the genre. Works such as Philidor's *Le Jardinier et son seigneur* (1761), Monsigny's *Le Deserteur* (1762), and Dalayrac's *Nina* (1786), brought the genre through a genesis that no longer existed solely to amuse. Opéra Comique now aimed to make the audience ponder the more humane and philosophical issues. Emotional content and thought-provoking plots become part of the new order, and the French Opéra Comique lends a springboard from which Singspiel will leap.

Mozart's *Die Zauberflöte* is without question the strongest example of the Singspiel tradition composed before or since its premiere. Mozart was not new to the Singspiel tradition, and his first attempt within the genre was in 1768. *Bastien und Bastienne*, composed when Mozart was 12, is treated as a parody on Rousseau's *Le Devin du village*. Other pre-*Die Zauberflöte* examples of Mozart's output in Singspiel include *Der Schauspieldirektor*, finished in 1786, the unfinished *Zaide* dating from 1780 and a certain pre-cursor to *Die Zauberflöte*: *Die Entfuhrung aus dem Serail* (1782). In the final vaudeville of *Die*

Entfuhrung aus dem Serail, a strong philosophical reference to the future Sarastro character is furnished: "Nothing is more odious than vengeance. On the contrary, to be humane, to have a good heart, and to pardon without personal resentment-that alone is characteristic of great souls."

Die Zauberflöte opened in Vienna on the evening of September 30, 1791. Mozart conducted the first two performances, when he was overtaken by his last illness. He lingered on while the opera had an unprecedented run of more than one hundred consecutive performances. It is said that in his sick bed, watch in hand, he would follow in imagination the performance of his work in the theatre. Then he died after its 67th performance.

The opera has been described as "an Enlightenment allegory, veiled in Masonic ritual". The story, founded on a fable by Wieland, is based upon circumstances connected with the mysterious worship of Isis, the deity of the ancient Egyptians. It is also a story and a text that is very flighty, improbable and full of absurdities. But the libretto is packed full of symbols and references to the actual rituals of Freemasonry, perhaps contributing to the confusion of all those unfamiliar with Freemasonry itself – still shrouded in secrecy as it is.

To the Viennese of that day, political symbolism was easily and broadly interpreted; they saw the opera's Queen of the Night as no one other than their own Empress Maria Theresa, the hero Tamino was seen to be the "good" Emperor Joseph and the heroine Pamina was the Austrian people itself.

This political symbolism, real or imagined, helped contribute to the eventual banning of Masonry in Austria. The Austrian government was becoming increasingly alarmed about treasonous sentiments, especially in the Masonic orders. Its secret police reported the names of high officials involved in the brotherhood. Not too much later, the young and inexperienced Francis II was easily swayed by his conservative advisors and in June of 1795 an order came down to close all Masonic lodges in the Empire.

Freemasonry ceased to exist in Austria for more than a century. But *Die Zauberflöte*, not only possibly Mozart's greatest piece of music – it is said to also contain every form of music, from lied to chorale to fugue – it has also remained synonymous with Masonic symbolism to this very day.

As for most operas, the plot of *Die Zauberflöte* is not easily summarized. When the First Act begins, we find ourselves in the wilderness, in a large forest. At the back is a circular or roundish temple. Tamino enters, pursued by a large serpent which is threatening to kill him. He faints, but as he does so, the doors of the temple open and three veiled ladies rush out to kill the beast with spears of silver (silver as reference to the moon, representing Isis); they represent the three spheres of the Sahu spirit (7, 8, 9), which are the realm of Isis ("country of the Queen of the Night"). A forest – a classic symbol of the unconscious; also a symbol of life itself, the tangled circumstances we frequently find ourselves in. Another forest which immediately comes to mind is the one in which Dante finds himself at the beginning of his *Divina Commedia*: he was also threatened by various wild animals. In fact this forest, this wilderness, is nothing other than Yesod – the Sphere of the Moon and of the unconscious, the power of connection – which is further borne out by the fact that the three veiled Ladies are servants of the Queen of the Night: they are Priestesses of the Moon, as witness their silver spears. Three, of course, being the number of the Great Mother, Binah: the black veils refer to the Veiled Isis.

Tamino, on the other hand, is a Prince – a young man, whose destiny is to succeed his father and become the Ruler of the Land. Seen microcosmically, a King (or a Queen, for that matter) is a balanced human being, in command of his own inner Kingdom and thereby of his own circumstances: he has achieved integration of his Lower and Higher Selves; he is a true Initiate in the deepest sense of the word. In other words, a Prince is someone who is still aspiring to all this: he is a candidate, seeking Initiation.

It is also very important to keep in mind that a Prince is an educated person. He has prepared himself for Kingship through studies in many fields and disciplines.

This is a prerequisite for a good ruler: only a person with knowledge can rule well; therefore, he who wants to be King must first educate himself. In the language of the Mysteries, this means that in order to become eligible for Initiation, it is necessary to have reached the point where one has mastered the exoteric sciences, which train our minds and give the tools to understand the inner knowledge. There must be some degree of inner balance, otherwise the inner teachings will not be perceived. Tamino is brave and knowledgeable; he has stamina and self-control. In fact, Tamino may be regarded as an image of the rational conscious mind itself, rather like "The Magician" of the Tarot. The Kabbalists of old called this aspect of the microcosm, Ruach. A modern-day term is the Ego. But right now Tamino, the conscious mind, is out of action, lying unconscious on the ground. The Three Ladies, after some debate, all decide to return to the temple to inform the Queen of the Night, so the Prince is just left there, but not for long.

A curious figure enters – Papageno, the Bird Catcher. In fact, it is difficult to tell whether he is human or not: he is covered in feathers, and in one place he talks about something being "so horrible it makes him moult"! His feathers are, in fact, not worn like a coat that can be taken off at will, but are part of him. He is actually part human, part bird or animal. Papageno is a simple soul, a good-natured, earthy character. He is not exactly what one would term an intellectual. He likes simple things; if he lived today, his intellectual pursuits would limit themselves to comic books, futile TV and a pint at the pub. As he enters, he sings a simple little tune, very typical of him.

He operates at an instinctual level, and it is not surprising to learn that he is employed by the Temple of the Moon where he, in exchange for the birds he catches, is given wine, figs and sponge-cake – all sweet and pleasurable things. Papageno is much more interested in good food than in danger and adventure: he is basically a coward, has absolutely no self-control, he rarely stops to think at all, but there is nothing evil in him; he is the personification of the instincts, that part of the Ruach (the Ego) which Kabbalists term the Nefesch or the animal soul, that part of us that connects us to Nature. It is interesting to note that he carries a set of pipes, a Pan Flute.

As the story goes along, it is possible to note that all the characters may be regarded as aspects of one person: Tamino and Papageno are one. Tamino is the conscious mind of the person that is to be initiated; Papageno is his unconscious animal soul. He is the Nefesch part of the Ruach, for the instincts can never entirely be separated from the Ego. Treating persons in a drama or a myth as sub-personalities can often reveal very interesting things.

Tamino regains consciousness and assumes that Papageno is the one who has saved him from the serpent, something Papageno doesn't particularly mind: in fact, he takes full credit for it – very typical of the Nefesh, the instinctual level! However, the Three Ladies return and put a padlock on his mouth, "to teach him not to lie to strange people, and to stop him from bragging about heroic deeds done by others". So this scene represents the Yesodic subconscious level disciplining the instincts. Training such as this comes from many levels, not just the conscious one. In fact, the instincts are much better disciplined by the unconscious than by the conscious mind.

The Three Ladies then present Prince Tamino with a small portrait of the daughter of the Queen of the Night. And of course it's love at first sight – what else, especially since her name is "Pamina", a simple variation on his own name, Tamino. This shows the basic unity between the two. Pamina can be regarded as an aspect of himself which he has to reclaim in order to reach maturity and integration. In fact, Pamina is his contrasexual image – or to use a Jungian term, his 'anima'.

It is it not surprising, then, when we learn from the Three Priestesses that Pamina has been abducted by a powerful evil sorcerer – the anima is in a fallen, captive state. Naturally, Tamino promptly swears that he will save her.

At this point, the scenery suddenly changes: it becomes dark, and the Queen of the Night appears. She is sitting on a silver throne, decorated with silver stars. Under her feet is a silver crescent. You will note that the imagery used by Mozart and Schikaneder is very similar to that in the tarot card of "The High Priestess", which is not very surprising: there are strong links between this card, the Moon and the Goddess. Up until now we have encountered her in her Triple form, as the Three Ladies, but now she reveals herself fully as the Star-Crowned Isis of the Moon, of the subconscious, of Yesod. In a slow, plaintive aria, she tells Tamino that if he saves Pamina from the evil magician, Sarastro, he will then be free to marry her. Then she disappears, and the scenery changes back to normal, leaving Tamino wondering if it was a vision or a dream – so typical of an encounter with the astral levels of Yesod where everything is fluid and dreamlike.

The Three Ladies remove Papageno's padlock. He promises never to lie again. Tamino is given a magic flute with protective properties to help him on his rescue mission. Papageno, not wanting to get involved, decides that this is a probably a good time to vanish, but the Ladies stop him, saying that the Queen has decreed that he is to follow Tamino to Sarastro's castle. Understandably, he is not too happy about this, but agrees when he is given a set of silver bells, also with magical properties.

Tamino and Papageno are also assigned Three Guides to show them the way to Sarastro's castle:

> Three boys will hover near you on your journey;
> They will be your guides,
> Follow only their advice.

These three boys, hovering nearby, are the Guardian Angels of Tamino and Papageno. They are three in number for the sake of consistency, and also because they are assigned to watch over them by the Temple of the Queen of the Night, and as children they symbolise the purity of the Higher Self.

We might also regard them as personifications of the Tifaret[21] consciousness which now has

---

[21] *Sephirot* are the 10 attributes/emanations of the Kabbalistic tree of life, through which Ein

begun to overshadow, or "hover over", the person who is to be initiated, even if that person does not realize it. This is always the case when we are reaching the stage where initiation takes place – the Higher Consciousness will overshadow us to a certain extent, but very often it isn't until long afterwards that we recognize this fact. And in yet another and third sense, in the early stages the mystical consciousness is like a child, requiring care, love and protection.

The next scene, which is very brief, is in Sarastro's palace. Slaves are laughing, because Pamina has escaped from her jailer, Monostatos who plays the "double" of Tamino`s Higher Self, the dark Hero, the *Doppelgänger*, the shadow of the Higher Self. His name could be taken to mean "of a single state", "Single-minded" or perhaps "One-Track minded". He is a Moor – in other words, he is black. Monostatos is a cruel, embittered person who lusts after Pamina and is just about to rape her

---

Sof (The Infinite) reveals himself and continuously creates both the physical realm and the chain of higher metaphysical realms. Tifaret, the sixth, has the common association of "Spirituality", "Balance", "Integration", "Beauty", "Miracles", and "Compassion".

when he suddenly sees Papageno through a window. Frightened by one another's appearance — "surely this is the Devil" — they both run off in opposite directions.

Microcosmically speaking, Monostatos can perhaps be said to represent the Shadow, the complex of repressed psychic material in our subconscious or, using an old Mystery term, the dreaded Dweller on the Threshold.

Modern people cannot but help come up against the idea of racism here. One should keep in mind that 200 years ago, the so-called supremacy of the white races was rarely questioned. Therefore, it is very interesting to note that Schikaneder and Mozart have assigned an aria to Monostatos in which he sings, "skin colour matters not when one is in love". This might, perhaps, be seen as a reflection of the Masonic ideals of the essential brotherhood of all humankind.

After this short scene follows the Finale of the first act. The Three Genii, have guided Tamino to the gates of Sarastro's temple complex. The layout is interesting: we see three portals. The left one leads to the Temple of Reason, the right one to the Temple of Nature, and in the middle, another portal leads to the Temple of Wisdom.

The action started in the forest of Yesod, in front of the Temple of the Moon. We are still in Yesod, but Tamino is getting ready to leave the Sphere of the Moon, and on the Tree of Life there are three paths leading upwards from Yesod: the 30th Path, leading to Hod;[22] the 28th Path, which leads to Netzach,[23] and the 25th Path, leading to Tifaret. It just happens that these three paths correspond exactly to the three Temple Gates: In Hod is the Temple of Reason, of course; in Netzach is the Temple of Nature, and in Tifaret, which is the Sphere of the Sun, the Higher Self and of Higher Initiation, is the Temple of Wisdom! One begins to wonder if Schikaneder wasn't, after all, familiar with the Kabbalah!

Anyway, Tamino, who is of course firmly set upon rescuing Pamina from the evil sorcerer, Sarastro, boldly knocks on the right portal. From beyond it a chorus of priests replies "Stand back!". Puzzled, he tries the left one, with the same result: "Stand back!". He then

---

[22] The eighth Sephirah; in the Hebrew the word means "majesty" or "splendor" and denotes "praise" as well as "submission".

[23] The seventh Sephirah; it generally translates to "Eternity" and in context of Kabbalah refers to "Perpetuity", "Victory", or "Endurance".

tries the middle portal, and an old priest appears.

He asks him, "Where are you bound for, bold stranger? What do you seek in this holy place?" Tamino answers, "That which is love's and virtue's".

The priest replies, "Those are noble words – But how are you to find it? You are not guided by love and virtue, because you are inflamed by death and revenge."

Now, at this point something very interesting happens. Tamino, and the audience, discover that Sarastro is no evil-doer at all, but a Priest of the Sun, a Holy Man, and that the Queen of the Night is a false and treacherous woman who has plotted against him. Sarastro has indeed abducted Pamina from her mother, but only in order to protect Pamina from her mother's evil influence.

This might sound a bit puzzling, and it has indeed puzzled musicologists since *Die Zauberflöte* was first performed, but it is in a way typical of the reversal of values that is said to take place as we leave the subjective consciousness of Yesod, the Moon-consciousness, and enter the objective solar consciousness of Tifaret. Tamino is simply advancing on his path of initiation. He is leaving the shadowy, ever-shifting world of Yesod, and is preparing to fully enter the higher consciousness of Tifaret.

The priest has left Tamino at the gate. In despair he asks if Pamina is still alive, and a hidden chorus of priests reply "Pamina still lives!" He decides to play his flute – perhaps its magic will lead him to her – and after a few moments he hears Papageno's pipes in reply. Pamina and Papageno use the enchanted bells to escape from Monostato's slaves, and then join Tamino at the portal of the Temple of Wisdom.

A procession appears: Sarastro comes riding a chariot, drawn by six lions - the symbolism of this is perfectly obvious: six is the number of Tifaret; lions are solar symbols as well as symbols of royalty. Sarastro is indeed a Priest-King, in fact, his name is probably an allusion to Zoroaster (or "Zarathustra"), which further underlines his essential solar nature. There is no doubt about it: all this symbolism shows us that Sarastro is the Higher Self, or, as Kabbalists term it, the Neschamah.

Sarastro sentences Monostatos to receive 77 strokes of the bastinado. Tamino and Papageno are taken into the Temple of Trial to be purified, and the First Act ends with a chorus:

When virtue and justice
have strewn the path of the great with glory,
Then will the earth be the kingdom of heaven
And mortals will be like gods!

The second act begins with another march as the College of Priests process into a courtyard inside the Temple of the Sun. There is a grove of palm trees – symbols of victory – with golden leaves. There is reason to assume that the palm trees stand in for akacias, which have a deep symbolic significance within Freemasonry. There are also 18 seats or sieges. On each siege stands a pyramid and a large black horn, set in gold: the 18 four-sided pyramids make a total of 72 sides, which is the number of the Schemhamforasch – the Great Name of God, which is inextricably linked to the Rosicrucian Mysteries. Each priest is holding a palm (read, akacia) twig in his hand. Sarastro opens the meeting, saying:

> Brethren! Initiates of the Temple of Wisdom; Servants of Isis and Osiris! Tamino, who is waiting at the Northern Gate of the Temple, is yearning to be free of the veil of the night, he wants to behold the sanctuary of Light.

It's spelled out for us here: the candidate is about to raise his consciousness from the shadowy realms of Yesod to Tifaret, where the Sun never sets, where, in fact, the Sun can be seen at Midnight.

We also learn that Pamina is destined for Tamino, and that this is the real reason for her abduction from the Queen of the Night, who is described as being full of deceit, seeking to mislead the people with illusion and superstition – glamour or maya – typical properties of an unbalanced Yesod.

The Moon Temple is served only by women, and the Sun Temple only by men. Thus, what we have got here is actually a polarity between the Moon and the Sun, between the subconscious and the conscious – and the Age of Enlightenment was very much in favour of the conscious mind as a guiding principle. Remember, the previous period of political and spiritual unrest (religious wars, witch hunts, etc.) had indeed proved to be a time of "lunacy" (and the word "lunacy" is derived from the Latin name for the Moon, Luna). Therefore, Reason, as symbolised by the Sun, was perceived as the only alternative.

However, we also learn that Sarastro is Pamina's father! Thus she is, in fact, the daughter of the Moon and the Sun: pure alchemy. And by the way, during the priestly deliberations we hear, three times, the initiation trombones sound their three-chord fanfare.

Meanwhile, Tamino and Papageno are brought into a dark chamber by two priests. They will later realize that they are blind. This refers to the fact that spiritual things cannot be perceived with the five senses. Papageno is afraid. Solemnly the first priest asks them: "Strangers, what do you seek or demand of us?" Tamino answers: "Friendship and love". He is willing to undergo any ordeal, no matter how painful, in order to win Pamina. Now the other priest questions Papageno about his ideals and hears, to his displeasure, that he is not at all anxious to acquire wisdom; all he wants is sleep, food and drink, and if only it were possible, a pretty young wife, but that he does not intend to undergo ordeals and mortal danger to this end: "I think I'll stay single". On being promised a young pretty Papagena who matches him in everything, he is prepared to at least attempt the ordeal of silence.

They are told that they will be left alone, and that no matter what happens, they may not speak. If they do, all is lost. The first test is to be able to resist the guiles of women: this is the beginning of wisdom.

To modern ears this sounds decidedly sexist, so let's rephrase it slightly. The beginning of wisdom is to be able to liberate oneself from being dominated by the forces of the subjective and subconscious mind as represented by the Moon. It also has to do with controlling one's sexuality; the Initiate is not ruled by his passions. There is nothing wrong with having passions, not at all, but to advance on the Path, your passions must not control the mind, the human being must rule over them; one must not suppress them, but rule them wisely. Also, Tamino and Papageno are not being told to give up women: it is a simply a test, and as such is limited in time. Neither are women decried anywhere in the text, nor is the female principle. The discussion is simply based on aspects of the soul. It has nothing to do with physical gender.

Suddenly, the Tree Ladies appear "from below the stage", which symbolizes the "subconscious", seemingly out of nowhere. They try everything in order to make Tamino and Papageno speak to them. Papageno, who has no self-control, can barely keep himself from talking; Tamino constantly has to tell him to shut up. Finally, a chorus of Initiates proclaims: "The holy threshold has been desecrated! Away with the women to Hell!" The Ladies vanish, but the Queen of Night is still at large in the Temple. She is furious because Tamino has chosen to become an Initiate of the Sun. She appears in her daughter's chamber and calls upon her to kill Sarastro and to hand her the powerful Disc of the Sun. Otherwise she will forever be disowned. So, the forces of Night are indeed threatening to overtake the Realms of the Sun.

So, an uprush of subconscious force, working through the anima of the candidate, is threatening to flood the conscious mind, thereby cutting off all contact with the superconscious levels of Tifaret. It is in fact a classic reaction from the subconscious: it does not want to change, it wants to stay the way it is, and it will go to great lengths to prevent any change in consciousness. This applies to quite mundane things, like giving up smoking, and it also applies to Initiation. Here, though, we see it in a very dramatic and extreme form: by acquiring the Disc of the Sun, the subconscious would overthrow the superconscious and rule supreme — a very serious mental condition, if not a total dissolution of the entire psyche.

But of course, the Higher Self cannot be killed. When the Queen of the Night has vanished, Sarastro appears, comforting Pamina: "in these halls no traitors can lurk, for here we all forgive our enemies." Very typical of the Higher Self, which is one with all other Higher Selves.

Meanwhile, it's time for the Tamino's and Papageno's second trial which again consist of silence. The two priests lead them into a vast hall; one of them mentions that failure in this trial is punished with "lightning and thunder", which is the scientific hint, because Jupiter is a planet with intense electrical activity, it is constantly covered with thousands of storms of thunder and lightning. Papageno chatters and complains that he is hungry. Their Guardian Angels, the Three Boys, appear from on high bringing the Magic Flute and the Magic Bells. They also bring a table full of food – Papageno immediately proceeds to overeat. Tamino plays his flute, and Pamina is attracted by its sounds. Tamino turns away, since he has been forbidden to speak. Pamina cannot understand this and thinks Tamino has stopped loving her. This is the second test, one which Tamino just barely is able to pass. Papageno doesn't notice: he's too busy chewing. Then the trombones call on the two men to continue on their way.

Sarastro praises Tamino for his calm. Pamina, who by now is quite beside herself and even has contemplated suicide, is brought in. Sarastro bids the two say farewell, for it is time for the final test.

Papageno, meanwhile, has lost his way. He can't pass into the next hall: wherever he goes, he hears "Stand back!" One of the priests arrives and rebukes him, telling him that if he goes on like this, he will never attain to the celestial joy of the Initiates. This doesn't bother Papageno a bit: what he'd like just now is a glass of wine. And as he wishes, so it is.

Tamino is ready to undertake the third and final test: the Trial by Water and Fire. Once again, the key switches to the Masonic key of E flat major. We can see two mountains on either side of the stage: through two openings can be seen black mist and glowing fire, respectively. Two men in black armour, wearing helmets with burning crests, read from a pyramid:

He who treads the road full of care,
Is purified by fire, water, air and earth.
If he can overcome the fear of death,

he soars heavenwards away from earth!
Enlightened, he will then be able
To dedicate himself entirely to the mysteries of Isis.

The two men's hymn is one of the most evocative passages in the opera: very suitable, by the way, for Lodge initiations.

Just as Tamino is about to enter the first cave, he hears the voice of Pamina, who has been given permission to join him as an Initiate: they can now undergo the final test together. It is important to notice that the Sun temple is a male temple, a temple of the Sun: only men are allowed as Initiates. By letting Tamino and Pamina undergo the tests as one unit – a syzygy – both principles are joined together. This is a sure proof of balance and of a successful initiation.

They pass through the portal, which closes behind them. The music during the actual test is very quiet: Tamino plays his magic flute, accompanied only by soft trombones and kettle drums.

The audience is not allowed to see the actual tests – they remain secret and withdrawn – but finally Tamino and Pamina emerge from the cave and the stage transforms into a brightly lit hall. A chorus greets them triumphantly and bids them enter the Temple as full Initiates.

This is basically the whole story. After this, the Queen of the Night and Monostatos make an abortive attempt to storm the Sun Temple: but of course the Sun cannot be conquered; the Queen of the Night and her followers are thrown into the abyss, and immediately the stage transforms into a gigantic Sun. Sarastro announces the sun's triumph over the night. Tamino and Pamina are now wearing priestly robes. They are surrounded by Egyptian priests on either side, and the Three Boys are holding flowers in their hands. Everyone praises the courage of Tamino and Pamina in enduring their trials, gives thanks to Isis and Osiris and hails the dawn of a new era of wisdom and brotherhood:

> Hail to you who are blest!
> You came through the night!
> Thanks! Thanks! Thanks be to you, Osiris!
> And thanks be to you, Isis!
> Strength has conquered
> And crowned as a reward
> Beauty and Wisdom
> With an everlasting crown!

As for Papageno, he never became an initiate, having chosen the wine instead (what else would one expect from the instincts?). He despairs at having lost Papagena and decides to hang himself. The three child-spirits appear and stop him. They advise him to play his magic bells to summon Papagena. She appears and, united, the happy couple stutter in astonishment. They plan their future and dream of the many children they will have together. So everybody was happily mated, each principle of the soul on its own level: Papageno – the instincts – "marries" Papagena; Tamino – the conscious mind – "marries" Pamina, the Anima; and the Higher Self, Sarastro, through whom all of this came about, watches over them all... he is the King that Tamino is destined to succeed, in a higher initiation still!

Taken as a whole *Die Zauberflöte* symbolizes much more of the journey of spiritual evolution of the newly-made Mason, however, or perhaps even that of all of Mankind. From the very first moments, when Tamino is menaced by the snake, we are invited to consider how man begins his existence. The snake may be taken as a symbol of ignorance, ready to devour even the aristocrat, such as Tamino, as well as the common people (the similarity of the snake to that of the dragon in the opening cantos of Spenser's *The Faerie Queen*, where the monster represents Error is not necessarily coincidental). The rescue from the symbol of ignorance is affected, however, by the forces of superstition. Some commentators identify the Queen of the Night with Lilith, the mythical first wife of Adam, who rejected God and became a demon of the night, attempting to entrap the souls of men by seduction. Tamino and Papageno indeed fall victim to the Queen's blandishments and succeed in "rescuing" Pamina by stealth.

Wisdom is not to be gained by dishonest means, however, and Tamino fortunately addresses the guardians of Wisdom's Temple candidly in his desire for a direct confrontation with Sarastro. It is then that the trickery worked on the searchers becomes clear. This scene teaches that while superstition may appeal of itself to one who is ignorant, those in the grip of false beliefs must choose to free themselves by their own actions. The relationship to the requirement to seek Masonic membership voluntarily is apparent. Sarastro makes clear to Tamino and Papageno how they have been victimized. Desiring further enlightenment, they are at once plunged into darkness, a phenomenon that will surprise no Mason.

It is not necessary to elaborate on the committee that considers Tamino's application for admission to the Temple of Wisdom nor on the trials of darkness, silence, circumspection, privation, and even fire and water that he must undergo; their meaning is quite transparent. But it is worth looking further into the character of Papageno, who accompanies Tamino into the chamber of reflection and there experiences some of the same tests. Papageno fails these tests miserably, but surprisingly is rewarded nonetheless. What conclusions are we to draw from this paradox? It is that Papageno differs significantly from Monostatos or the Queen of the Night in a most important way: he has at least endeavored to seek wisdom and climb above his simple and ignorant origins among the beasts of the field and the birds of the air. The Queen of the Night wishes to enslave all; Papageno desires at least freedom for himself. Monostatos would seize Pamina by force; Papageno hopes for a wife of his own to be given him. Despite his inability to pass the severe tests required for a disciple of wisdom, Papageno makes one vital decision: he chooses to be led by those who have acquired wisdom. From this comes his entitlement to earthly reward, if not celestial illumination. As the higher degrees of Masonry speak to the duties of the sagacious to provide wise leadership, there is also a duty incumbent upon the masses, who themselves may be unable to accept the stern demands of wisdom, at least to choose enlightened leaders. When the masses seek immediate gratification by setting above them those who rule in the name of ignorance and superstition, the misery of all is the inevitable result.

The librettist used a variety of Masonic sources for the libretto, in particular, the Abbe Terrasson novel *Sethos*, "which was a great influence in French Freemasonry... and continued to play a role in Freemasonry to the end of the 19th Century."[24]

This text focuses on Freemasonry's relationship with the ideology of ancient Egyptian religions. Parallels between this book and *Die Zauberflöte* include Terrasson's power seizing Queen Dalucca – highly reminiscent of the opera's Queen of the Night – and the high Priest, a character similar to Sarastro.[25] The

---

[24] NETTL PAUL, *Mozart and Masonry*, New York: Philosophical Library, p. 72, 1957.

[25] Ibid, p. 73.

relevance of the 18 priests at the start of the second act becomes apparent when you learn that "Eighteen priests kept watch over Hiram's grave and the number of priestesses who performed sacrifices in Sethos is also eighteen."[26] The conflicting desires of love and initiative are also present in the novel,[27] and musicologist Rodney Milnes points out a string of other similarities. "From Sethos comes the text recited by the Armed Men, the Three Ladies, the serpent, the trials of fire and water, and the ritual of the second Act",[28] not to mention Sarastro's opening air from Act II, which is "taken practically word for word."[29]

The extensive use of this source and others like it helped steep the libretto in Masonic ideology. As Dent explains, "The moral sentiments [...] were drawn largely from Masonic teaching [...] (such as) the importance assigned to manliness and friendship, to the se-

---

[26] Ibid, p. 74.

[27] Ibid, p. 78.

[28] MILNES RODNEY, *'Singspiel and Symbolism' in The Magic Flute*, ed. N. John, London: John Calder, 1980, 2nd edition, p. 14.

[29] DENT E. J., *Mozart's Operas: A Critical Study*, Oxford: Oxford University Press, 1947, 2nd edition, p. 227.

crecy of the mystic rites."[30] The main theme of the opera is the "journey from darkness to light",[31] as experienced by the character of Tamino – ultimately, the opera "celebrates the possibility of progress".[32] This is clearly an endorsement of the ideology of Freemasonry. The Queen of Night represents the darkness – her world is steeped in irrationality and superstition, described by music historian David Cairns as "the domain of ignorance and unregenerate women".[33] This is why the priest Sarastro is viewed as an enchanter – "the change he works in men [...] is a mere question of magic, and the flute likewise is a purely magical piece of property".[34]

Alternatively, Sarastro and his "noble brotherhood"[35] represent the masons and "the light of understanding",[36] where the human soul

---

[30] Idem, p. 223.

[31] MILNES RODNEY, *op. cit.*, p. 16.

[32] Ibidem.

[33] CAIRNS DAVID, *"A Vision of Reconciliation" in The Magic Flute*, ed. N. John, London: John Calder, 1980, 2nd edition, p. 19.

[34] Idem, p. 84.

[35] GUTMAN R.W., *Mozart: A Cultural Biography*, London: Seker & Warburg, 2000, p. 724.

[36] CAIRNS DAVID, *op. cit.*, p. 23.

"and all its former contradictions, and all it parts, having shed their negative aspects, are united into a single harmonious whole".[37] Like the Freemasons, the brotherhood has a Sprecher, or an orator. Their temples are called Nature, Reason and Wisdom, the three 'Lesser Lights' of Freemasonry,[38] and many people believe that the character of Sarastro is actually based on Ignaz Edler von Born, a "famous freemason and scholar".[39] Furthermore, Rodney Milnes argues that the Queen of Night and her conflict with Sarastro over "control of the Circle of the Sun symbolises the conflict on Masonic lore between the dualism proposed by inscriptions on the twin pillars of Hiram's Temple of Solomon."[40] These feature such opposing forces as "Masculine/Feminine, Sun/Moon, Fire/Water, Day/Night".[41]

Freemasons believe in the path of understanding and light. As the Genii – "beyond the dualism and thus perfect beings"[42] – sing,

---

[37] Ibidem.

[38] NETTL PAUL, *op. cit.*, p. 89.

[39] Idem, p. 84.

[40] MILNES RODNEY, *op. cit.*, p. 15.

[41] Ibidem.

[42] Ibidem.

'Soon superstition will vanish and wisdom triumph; come, Peace, and fill the hearts of men, so that earth will become a paradise and mortal men as the Gods themselves.' This is the principle hope of both the opera and Freemasonry in general.

Like all Freemasons, Tamino must undergo trials in order to join the brotherhood – "the tests by fire and water, which are found in *Sethos* as well as the masonic initiation."[43] He must gain enlightenment through hardship, just as Mozart had had to – through "suffering, self-sacrifice and love."[44] As in the Freemasons' initiation, Tamino is offered the chance to turn back, and is warned to remain secret and silent.[45] He also has to learn the masonic ideal of rejecting fear of death – "that fear of death which masonry had taught Mozart to overcome."[46] As Sarastro says, in the event of Tamino's death, "Then he will go to join Isis and Osiris and share their happiness before we do."[47]

---

[43] NETTL PAUL, *op. cit.*, p. 90.

[44] CAIRNS DAVID, op. cit., p. 24.

[45] NETTL PAUL, *op. cit.*, p. 90.

[46] DENT E. J., *op. cit.*, 253.

[47] MOZART W.A., *Die Zauberflotescore*, London: Barenreiter, 1960.

Numbers play an interesting role in *Die Zau-berflöte*. First, of course, they are the symbolic references to Freemasonry. Hermetic, alchemical, gematria,[48] and the Golden Section[49] are some of the applications. Of major importance are the numbers 3, 5 and 7, and additives, multiples, and combinations of these.

As follows, a brief analysis of the above-mentioned numbers:

NUMBER THREE

- ✓ Of the five human senses, the three which are the most important in Masonic symbolism are Seeing, Hearing, and Feeling, because of their respective

---

[48] A Jewish system of numerology that assigns numerical value to a word or phrase, in the belief that words or phrases with identical numerical values bear some relation to each other, or bear some relation to the number itself as it may apply to a person's age, the calendar year, or the like.

[49] An Assyro-Babylonian system of numerology later adopted by Jews which assigns numerical value to a word or phrase, in the belief that words or phrases with identical numerical values bear some relation to each other, or bear some relation to the number itself as it may apply to a person's age, the calendar year, or the like.

reference to certain modes of recognition, and because, by their use, Freemasons are enabled to practice that universal language the possession of which is the boast of the Order;

✓ There are, in the basic Lodge, three degrees: Entered Apprentice, Fellowcraft and Master Mason;

✓ There are three major officers in the basic Lodge: The Worshipful (that is, 'Respected') Master, the Senior Warden, and the Junior Warden. (These are the three officers with the gavels);

✓ The initiation ritual discusses both Three Greater Lights of Masonry and Three Lesser Lights of Masonry;

✓ There are three "burning tapers" arranged around the Altar that is at the center of every American Lodge room. (These may be actual tapers, but more commonly they are artfully formed stands with electric lights on top);

✓ The ritual mentions three "tenets" (principles) of Freemasonry;

✓ There are three symbolic moral pillars mentioned in the ritual;

✓ Traditionally, in older Masonic documents, the period of abbreviation is re-

placed by The "tripod," that
is, three dots arranged in an
equilateral triangle;

- ✓ The Holy Trinity, a perfect whole having beginning, middle and end;
- ✓ The three virtues of faith, hope and love/charity;
- ✓ The third letter of the Hebrew alphabet (G) as a Masonic symbol for God.

The opera begins in E flat – which has three flats in its key signature, forming the shape of a "tripod" – and opens with three detached chords.

Ouverture

These reoccur throughout the overture and the opera (*i.e.* triadic melody construction and repetitions of chords), sometimes in dotted rhythms, representing "a stylised version of the Entered Apprentice's knocking.[50]

The number three also recurs in a serpent cut into three pieces, three Ladies serving the Queen of Night, three genii working in Sarastro's realm, three slaves, the 18 (six times three) priests. Also, inscriptions upon the three temples refer to "Nature", "Reason" and "Wisdom", also obviously of Masonic origin – as are other references to armor, silver, gold, chariots and the final defeat of evil by the powers of light. Furthermore, the March of the Priests features a threefold sequence of eight note phrases. Similarly, the Fugato

---

[50] NETTL PAUL, *op. cit.*, p. 91.

106

theme of the Overture, with its pounding rhythms, is said to be a depiction of "working on the rough stone."[51]

In combinations of 3s, there is the use of the number 18, in the reference to the Scottish Rite degree of the Sovereign Rose Croix – already in existence and known in Mozart's time. The association with Blue Lodge Masonry is clear: upon being raised in the work of the third degree the candidate becomes a Master Mason. But beyond the third degree of Blue Lodge Masonry are upper degrees in two possible tracks, the York Rite or the Scottish Rite. The pelican feeding her young with her blood is a prominent symbol of the Ancient and Accepted Scottish Rite, and was adopted as such from the fact that the pelican, in ancient Christian art, was considered as the em-

---

[51] Ibidem.

blem of the Savior. Now this symbolism of the pelican, as a representative of the Savior, is almost universally supposed to be derived from the common belief that the pelican feeds her young with her blood, as the Savior shed his blood for mankind. The number 18 is obviously a multiple of 3 (3 x 3 x 2) and is applied in Die Zauberflöte in several ways: Sarastro enters in the 18th scene of Act I; there are 18 seats and 18 priests in the conclave at the beginning of Act II; the trials of fire and water occur in the 18th scene of Act II (in which the chorale tune begins in the pick-up to the 18th measure); Tamino's first measure of singing is in the 18th measure of the opening scene of Act I. This last point may seem pedestrian until we consider that the normal phrase length in Mozart's time would be in multiples of 4, so we would more likely expect an entrance on measure 16, not 18.

NUMBER FIVE

- ✓ Among the Pythagoreans, five was a mystical number, because it was formed by the union of the first even number and the first odd, rejecting unity; and hence it symbolised the mixed conditions of order and disorder, happiness and misfortune, life and death. The same union of the odd and even, or male and female, numbers made it the symbol of marriage;

✓ The number five consists of two unequal parts, 2 and 3. The diversity brings evil and misfortune. It symbolizes the individual (one who defies the natural order and is punished), the five fingers on the hand, the pentagram;

✓ It is the symbol of human microcosm. In the true pentacle, it is possible to see how the head, arms, and legs of a person standing spread eagled are 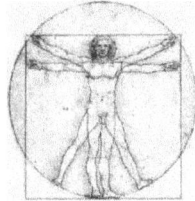 represented by the points of the star;

✓ In Freemasonry, five is a sacred number, inferior only in importance to three and seven. It is especially significant in the Fellow Craft's Degree, where five are required to hold a Lodge, and where, in the winding stairs, the five steps are referred to the orders of architecture and the human senses. In the Third Degree we find the reference to the five points of fellowship and their Symbol, the five-pointed star, symbolizing the ability of the will to control the elements: Spirit, Water, Fire, Earth and Air;

✓ In Freemasonry it represents women, and "five note figures are prominent in the work in the scenes that take place… in the feminine domain".[52]

NUMBER SEVEN

✓ The number 7 represents the seeker, the thinker, the searcher of hidden Truths, who knows that nothing is exactly as it seems and that reality is often hidden behind illusions;

✓ It refers to natural phenomena such as moon phases, number of planets and metals of early science;

✓ It is represented in numerous occurrences in the opera. The seventh eighth-note of the Allegro section of the Overture is marked forte and begins a turning figure, breaking up the repetition of a single pitch; this rhyth-

---

[52] CAIRNS DAVID, *op. cit.*, p. 19.

mic pattern occurs 'three' times in each of the statements of the fugue-like subject before the entrance of the next voice. Moreover, there is a sforzando on the third eighth note of the counter-subject! Scales of seven pitches, upward and downward, permeate the opera;

✓ The Golden Section can be determined in a number of passages in the opera, especially within sections in the Introduction (the opening scene, through the departure of the Three Ladies) and several arias and shorter pieces. For example, in the Queen's first-act aria, there are 103 measures in total; the Golden Section, measure 74, marks the beginning of the Queen's commission to Tamino to rescue Pamina (*Du, du, du wirst sie zu befreien gehen*). In the prayer to Isis and Osiris at the beginning of Act II, for Sarastro and men's chorus, the Golden Section marks the significant moment in which Sarastro refers to the descent to the grave should the candidate fail in his initiation (measure 35 of 56):

✓ Sarastro's power is bound up in the mystical seal of the seven circles of the sun.

Back to the overview of this chapter, Masonic ideology is also demonstrated by the music via the well-reasoned simplicity of Mozart's score, in terms of "form, style, material [...] yet it is a positive simplicity, subtle and purposeful, uncomplicated in its effect".[53] This is intended to evoke the calm rationality of the Freemasons. Symptomatic of this are the passages of block harmony he employs for "the expression of moral sentiments [...] to impress clearly onto the audience".[54] These effects are complemented with solemn instrumentation, such as in the finale of Act 1, where Tamino is guided to the Temple accompanied by "a solemn march, with soft pulsations of bassoons, trombones, muted trumpets and drums, and the gleam of flutes and clarinets in octaves".[55] With regards of trombones, in fact, Mozart draws special attention to this instrument. It's as if he wants to emphasize that they have a special function. Indeed, they do: throughout

---

[53] Idem, p. 17.

[54] DENT E. J., *op. cit.*, 245.

[55] DENT E. J., *op. cit.*, p. 26.

the rest of the opera, fanfares or chords for the 'three' trombones announce the next stage or phase of the process of initiation. They urge the protagonists on, they make things happen. Trombones are extremely ancient instruments. The name is Italian for "large trumpet", but whereas trumpets are martial instruments – having to do with the forces of Mars: energy, courage, war, and so forth – the trombones, on the other hand, are particularly royal instruments. Traditionally, trombones and their ancestors were mainly used in religious ceremonies. They represented the majesty and divinity of the king; compared to the trumpets, their sound is heavier, calmer, more dignified and expansive: all qualities of Jupiter. So we might say that trumpets belong to the Sphere of Gevurah[56] on the Tree of Life, and trombones belong to the Sphere of Chesed.[57]

However, we might also put the trombones in Tifaret, the Royal Sephira above all others, the

---

[56] The fifth *Sephirot* known as "restraint," "strength", "judgment", "power", and "concealment".

[57] It is given the association of kindness and love, and is the first of the emotive attributes of the *sephirot*.

Sphere of the King. Tifaret is also the Sphere of Sacrifice and of Higher Initiation, and since *Die Zauberflöte* is an opera about initiation and the trombones are given the task of summoning the characters to their initiation, we can regard the trombones as symbols of Tifaret, the Sphere of the Sun and of the Higher Self.

The final chorus is also an example of this "with drums and trumpets prominent, singing of virtue and justice".[59] In addition to this, Mozart produces "humanitarian melodies [which possess] a wonderful mildness and purity, silently glowing with metaphysical warmth."[60]

An example of this is Sarastro's aria, *O Isis und Osiris*, featuring as it does "wide bass inter-

---

[58] MOZART W.A., *Die Zauberflöte*, Finale n.8, Larghetto.

[59] CAIRNS DAVID, *op. cit.*, p. 28.

[60] NETTL PAUL, op. cit., p. 91.

vals"[61] and "new sonority basset-horns, trombones, violas in two parts and cellos [...] to undermine the solemnity".[62]

O Isis und Osiris, schenket
der Weisheit Geist dem neuen Paar!
Die ihr der Wandr'er Schritte lenket,
Stärkt mit Geduld sie in Gefahr.
Laßt sie der Prüfung Früchte sehen,
Doch sollen sie zu Grabe gehen,
So lohnt der Tugend kühnen Lauf,
Nehmt sie in euren Wohnsitz auf.

O Isis and Osiris, give
the spirit of wisdom to the new pair!
She who links to her the wanderer's steps,
Strengthens them with patience in danger.
Let them see the fruits of the test,
But, if they should go to the grave,
Then, the valient course of virtue rewarded,
Receive them in your abode.

---

[61] Idem, 92.
[62] CAIRNS DAVID, *op. cit.*, p. 29.

Mozart also imbues the Masons with an appropriate air of mystery, such as we feel during the March of the Priests as a consequence of its interrupted cadences and mystical sounding ascending parallel sixths.

---

[63] MOZART W.A., *Die Zauberflöte*, n.10, Aria with chorus.

These appear again in the introduction to Sarastro's subsequent aria. This features a further enchanting effect whereby the chorus repeats the final phrase each half aria, distributed varyingly between the parts, evoking a fitting sense of ritual.

---

[64] MOZART W.A., *Die Zauberflöte*, n.9, March.

This sense of mystery is amplified by imaginative orchestral effects. For instance, when in the Finale of the first Act – where Tamino questions the orator – and "the basses are parallel to the voices, while the strings pulsate softly [...] (and) the voices answer from within, *Bald, Jüngling, oder nie* [Soon, soon, or never], one feels something of the mystical power which Freemasonry held over Mozart".[65]

---

[65] NETTL PAUL, *op. cit.*, p. 92.

This portrayal is all the more powerful when contrasted with the completely opposite portrayal of the Queen of Night, and her furiously passionate Italianate arias. These are brimming with wild coloratura and rapid phrases that dart back and forth, displaying her lack of reasoned understanding and calm logic.

Also of significance are the trials, which Mozart paints beautifully in order to emphasise the lengths the Masons go to for their beliefs. Particularly effective is the depiction of the trial by fire, with its "beating rhythms, the imitative treatment, the sobbing of the violins and the chromaticism."[66]

Given the story, the numerous symbols and Masonic references, and the musical treatments Mozart employs, it is important not to view Mozart's opera simply as a masonic treatise. Much more than that, Freemasonry is

---

[66] Ibidem.

used as a foundation stone from which the truly great elements of the opera spring – the philosophical doctrine of reason, the sublime music that evokes this, the richly developed libretto and finely realized characters, and Mozart's extraordinary instinct for such potent musical drama.

The early death of the composer Wolfgang Amadeus Mozart has fascinated the world for more than two centuries. The cause of the composer's demise remains a mystery. Historians, anthropologists, musicologists and doctors have debated this mystery in books, journals and conferences – and yet the solution eludes them. Meanwhile, the public, stirred by romantic imagination, wonders: was Mozart murdered, or was it disease that killed him?

On 20 November, 1791, during a fever epidemic, Wolfgang Amadeus Mozart unexpectedly took ill – developing a high fever, headache, sweats, and severe swelling and pain in his hands and legs. By the 14th day of his illness, his swelling had seriously worsened. With the swelling came nausea and vomiting, diarrhoea, a persistent rash and an abominable reek which rose from his body to greet his visitors.

Mozart died at one in the morning on 5 December 1791, at No. 4 Rauhensteingasse in Vienna: he suffered a convulsion, lapsed into a coma and died. He was 35. The building was demolished in 1849, but a plaque marks the spot today. The funeral arrangements were made by Mozart's friend and patron, Baron Gottfried van Swieten.

The most popular credited hypotheses are based on Masonry and the Italian composer Antonio Salieri. In the first case, some people believe that the Freemasons murdered Mozart because he revealed secrets about their organization in his opera, *Die Zauberflöte*. As acknowledged in the previous chapter, the Masons cared very much for Wolfgang, and he for them, as well. When the composer was having a financial crisis, at the end of the 1780s, and could not pay his bills, Michael Puchberg, the treasurer of Mozart's lodge, loaned him a considerable amount of money to make it through. Puchberg was a close friend of Mozart's, and after the composer died, he waited until his wife, Constanze, had regained her financial stability before asking for repayment. Upon his death, the lodge published a speech held at the funeral ceremony in Mozart's honor. They also printed one of his last pieces, *Kleine Freymaurer-Kantate* in score for Constanze's benefit.

Apart from the hoary theory about being killed for breaking his oath of secrecy by putting Masonic secrets in his opera, some have also suggested Mozart was in debt up to his eyeballs from gambling with lodge brothers, who may have gotten tired of waiting for repayment.

There is another Masonic conspiracy, of a sort, associated with Mozart's death. It seems he may have been dallying with Magdelena Hofdemel, his student, the 23-year-old wife of lodge brother Franz Hofdemel. Mozart, a notorious womanizer, had a steamy affair with her, and supposedly made her his mistress and got her pregnant. It is believed Franz found out about the affair, poisoned Mozart, and shortly after the funeral went home and hacked up the five-month pregnant Magdalena with a razor, then cut his own throat with the same razor. Magdalena survived the slashing and named her child after Mozart and her husband.

But the rumor was that Franz Hofdemel discovered the affair, and then poisoned Mozart as Step One of his murder/suicide plot. Magdelena's child was a walking billboard for Mozart's purported indiscretion, and Ludwig Von Beethoven, reputed to be a Vienna Freemason as well, refused to play in any venue Magdelena was attending.

A likely perpetrator of Mozart's death, however, remained unidentified until the autumn of 1823, when reports circulated that the Italian Antonio Salieri (1750-1825), rival composer, had become non compos mentis and unsuccessfully attempted suicide by slashing his throat.[67] Allegedly, he had confessed to poisoning Mozart, a rumor recorded in the "conversation books" of Ludwig van Beethoven (1770-1827), in which his interlocutors wrote their remarks to communicate with the deaf composer. Beethoven's nephew Karl stated, "Salieri maintains that he poisoned Mozart", and Anton Schindler, Beethoven's secretary and factotum, commented, "Salieri is very ill again. He is quite deranged. In his ravings he keeps claiming that he is guilty of Mozart's death and made away with him by poison".[68] Because Beethoven replied orally to the queries and comments that his visitors inscribed in his conversation books, his reaction to these allegations is unknown.

---

[67] Medical Journal Article: *What Killed Mozart?*, by Jan V. Hirschmann, MD, in Archives of Internal Medicine, Volume 161, June 2001, pp. 1381-1389.

[68] Idem.

In October 1823, however, Ignaz Moscheles, a pupil of Beethoven's and Salieri's, visited the latter in the hospital where he was confined:

> His appearance already shocked me and he spoke only in broken sentences about his imminent death. But at the end he said, "Although this is my last illness, I can assure you on my word of honor that there is no truth in that absurd rumor; you know that I was supposed to have poisoned Mozart. But no, it's malice, pure malice, tell the world, dear Moscheles, old Salieri, who will soon die, has told you".[69]

In August 1824, Giuseppe Carpani published a vigorous defense of his friend, Salieri, in an Italian journal. In it, he included a letter solicited from Dr. Eduard Guldener von Lobes, who had examined Mozart's body and found nothing awry, and he printed the testimony of two nurses who had cared for Salieri continuously from the winter of 1823.

They stated that no one but they and the physicians had seen the patient, and never had he confessed to poisoning Mozart.

---

[69] Idem.

Furthermore, a compelling motive remained unclear. In Vienna, Salieri, not Mozart, had been the court Kappelmeister, the emperor's chief musician. The Italian composer had greater wealth, a higher salary, and, as an opera composer, a reputation at least as great as Mozart's. Although the two competed and sometimes clashed, Mozart's last letter, written to Constanze on October 14, 1791, suggests a cordial relation at the time of his death. He had taken Salieri and Madame Cavalieri in his carriage to a performance of his opera, *Die Zauberflöte*, where they sat with Mozart in his box. Their response was gratifying:

> You cannot believe how polite they both were, – how much they liked not my music, but the libretto and everything. They both said that it was an operone [a grand opera], worthy to be performed for the grandest festival and before the greatest monarch, and that they would often go to see it, as they had never seen a more beautiful or delightful show. He [Salieri] listened and watched most attentively and from the overture to the last chorus there was not a single number that did not call forth from him a bravo! or bello! It seemed as if they could not thank me

enough for my kindness. (October 14th 1791)[70]

Possibly, Salieri's reactions were disingenuous, but Mozart obviously considered them sincere, even though he, like his father, was particularly suspicious of conspiracies and cabals against him, especially among the Italian composers. Moreover, according to one of his students, Salieri "did not harbor a grudge against Mozart, who eclipsed him. [...]".[71]

In 1830, the great Russian author Aleksandr Pushkin (1799-1837) wrote a short play, *Mozart and Salieri*, in which he accepted the poisoning theory and supplied novel motives envy and resentment: envy because of Mozart's palpably greater gifts and resentment because his accomplishments seemed effortless and his conduct childish. To Salieri, it is unjust that the sacred gift of immortal genius seems arbitrarily bestowed rather than being a reward for toil, devotion, prayer, and self-sacrifice. Part of Salieri's motive is to benefit his fellow

---

[70] CF. *The Cambridge Mozart Encyclopedia*, ed. by Cliff Eisen and Simon P. Keefe, Cambridge: Cambridge University Press, 2006, p. 552.

[71] Medical Journal Article: *What Killed Mozart?, op. cit..*

composers, who will welcome Mozart's death, for the achievements of his music have established exalted standards that others can never attain.

According to Niemetschek's biography, this view had a historical correlate:

> A composer [...] said to a colleague at Mozart's death, with much truth and uprightness: "Of course it's too bad about such a great genius, but it's good for us that he's dead. Because if he'd lived longer, really the world would not have given a single piece of bread for our compositions".[72]

The Russian composer Nicholai Rimsky-Korsakov (1844-1908) transformed Pushkin's work into an opera in 1898, and Peter Shaffer continued the theme of Salieri's envy and recognition of Mozart's superior talent in *Amadeus*, first as a play in 1979 and later, considerably altered, as a film in 1984, directed by Milos Forman. In Shaffer's work, Salieri, realizing that his own achievements and gifts are mediocre, resents that God has chosen Mozart (Amadeus: "beloved of God") to be His voice. Salieri does not poison Mozart

---

[72] Idem.

but, pretending to be an ally, sabotages his career. Disguised as the imposing messenger commissioning the *Requiem*, Salieri hastens Mozart's death by provoking him to finish this piece, even when obviously ill.

There is, however, far more evidence of a co-operative relationship between the two composers than one of real enmity. For example, Mozart's widow appointed Salieri to teach their son, Franz Xaver, and when Salieri was appointed Kapellmeister in 1788, he revived Figaro instead of bringing out a new opera of his own. In addition, when he went to the coronation festivities for Leopold II in 1790 he had no fewer than three Mozart masses in his luggage. In the late summer of 1785, Salieri and Mozart composed a cantata for voice and piano together, entitled *Per la ricuperata salute di Ophelia*, which celebrated the happy return to the stage of the famous singer Nancy Storace. This cantata has been lost, although it was published by Artaria in 1785. Mozart's *Davide penitente* K.469 (1785), his piano concerto in E flat major K.482 (1785), the clarinet quintet K.581 (1789) and the great symphony in G minor K.550 were all premiered at the suggestion of Salieri, who conducted a performance of the G minor symphony in 1791, the year of Mozart's death. In a nutshell, Salieri had no reason to murder Mozart; he was in a position of power and esteem with a handsome stipend, and Mozart was of little threat to him.

In most of the poisoning theories, the mysterious patron who commissioned the *Requiem* has a crucial role. His identity, however, later became apparent: he was Count Franz von Walsegg-Stuppach, a music lover and amateur composer, who regularly sponsored concerts at his castle; he had a reputation for commissioning works from talented composers and then passing them off as his own – hard to do when the true composer is still alive and living in the vicinity. His motives were dishonest but not sinister. On February 14, 1791, his 20-year-old wife had died, and he wished to have a Requiem played at each anniversary of her death. He instructed his attorney in Vienna to send a clerk to Mozart as his unidentified emissary, because, as he had done on other occasions with different composers, he wanted to commission the work anonymously and then present it as his own composition.

The poisoning theory, while tantalizing and lurid, loses its credibility in that Mozart's deathbed symptoms don't support the notion. Had arsenic been used, witnesses would have observed throat burning, difficulty swallowing, abdominal pain, difficulty breathing, delirium, sensorimotor abnormalities, and erythroderma; none of which were observed. Mercury would have led to memory loss, excessive salivation, tremors, delirium, and emotional oversensitivity, which were also not observed. This makes it more likely that Mozart died from causes other than poison.

Let's discuss, in the following pages, other relevant theories!

Australian musicologist, Otto Erich Deutsch (1883 - 1967), taught us that only the study of the authentic documents about a person could bring us nearer to the biographical truth. Since Mozart's death, there have been countless theories as to what constituted severe miliary fever. An autopsy was never performed on the composer, although Dr. Eduard Guldener von Lobes, who examined his body, found no evidence of foul play. Mozart was buried under the edicts of his time, so there are no bones or hair to analyze.

A physician, legally required to examine the body to exclude foul play, found nothing amiss but performed no autopsy. Regulations specified that interment not occur until 48 hours after death, apparently to ensure that no one was buried alive.[73] During that time, a service took place at St Stephen's Cathedral, where he and Constanze had wed nine years earlier, and probably on the night of December 7, during inclement weather, a hearse transported the corpse to a cemetery in St Marx, a village about 5 km outside Vienna.

Without ceremony or a priest in attendance, Mozart was interred, probably in a coffin in a simple grave. It was common practice, however, to sew the unclothed bodies of the dead in linen sacks, place several together in a communal pit, and cover them with quicklime to hasten decomposition. No permanent marker commemorated his burial site, and, about seven years later, workers dug up the grave and reused it, dispersing the remains.

These details have fostered the view that Mozart died destitute and unappreciated, with an ignominious funeral, but, in fact, the obsequies conformed to the edicts of the Habsburg monarch and Holy Roman Emperor, Joseph II, whose court was in Vienna. In 1784, this "enlightened despot," appalled by the extravagant cost and lavishness of funerals, had prohibited excessive displays and had decreed

---

[73] Idem.

that priests not attend the burial, which was to occur without pomp or ceremony. In addition, drivers of the hearses could convey the body to the cemeteries outside the city only at night, and they could not stop for drinks at taverns along the way, for fear that they would become intoxicated and unable to lead the horses to the appropriate destination. Although Joseph II died in 1790, his successor, Leopold II, had not rescinded these regulations.

Use of a single grave for up to five adults or four adults and two children was commonplace then, because the cemeteries, surrounded by walls, had such limited space.[74] Mozart's burial was not a pauper's, which the parish provided without charge. Instead, his widow purchased a third-class funeral, the least expensive and certainly the most common in Vienna. Only aristocrats and the wealthy could be interred in family tombs, which constituted a first-class funeral.

Second-class and third-class funerals, on the other hand, differed only in the church ceremony, choice of bells and music, and number of pallbearers.

---

[74] Idem.

Mozart did not die in obscurity. On December 7, 1791, a Vienna newspaper printed an editorial stating:

> Known from his childhood as the possessor of the finest musical talent in all Europe, through the fortunate development of his exceptional natural gifts and through persistent application he climbed the pinnacle of the greatest Masters; his works, loved and admired by all [...] are the measure of the irreplaceable loss that the noble art of music has suffered by his death.

The tribute was not just a provincial view: an account of a memorial concert in Prague on December 14, 1791, asserted that almost the entire city streamed toward the square, so that the Wälscher Platz could hardly accommodate all the carriages nor could the large church, which can house nearly 4000 persons, contain all the admirers of the composer.

At the time of his death, Mozart was not living in penury. He had had serious financial difficulties from 1788 to 1790, but the last year of his life was exceptionally remunerative. He lived well, but not extravagantly, and despite some debts, his prospects for increasing wealth were excellent.

The identification of Mozart's mysterious patron substantially undermines many of the conspiracy theories, but the plausibility of poisoning or any other explanation for Mozart's death depends mostly on analyzing the details of his illness.

Certain problems, however, undermine any attempt to establish the identity of an ailment that occurred in the distant past: the terminology and the concepts of disease, which partly determine what clinicians observe and the language that they use in medical discourse, have changed so extensively that understanding them now is difficult. Even when earlier clinicians rendered a diagnosis that remains in use today, they may have included under the rubric of a single disease several illnesses that resemble one another but are now considered distinct entities. Accordingly, it is hazardous to assume that the label applied to a disorder in the distant past is accurate by current standards. Because of alterations in the inciting agent or the host, the manifestations of a disease may have changed substantially. Until relatively recently, clinicians lacked many of the diagnostic techniques now considered fundamental.

French physician René Laennec (1781-1826) devised the stethoscope and described lung and cardiac auscultation in 1819. German physician Ludwig Traube (1818-1876) introduced the clinical use of the thermometer in the 1850s, and Carl Wunderlich (1815-1877) in 1868 determined the normal range of body temperature. Any mention of fever in Mozart's illness, therefore, rested on a subjective assessment, rather than an actual measurement. A practical sphygmomanometer became available only in the late 19th century. Therefore, clinicians in the late 1700s did not have the techniques to record the vital signs of temperature and blood pressure or the equipment to listen to heart and lungs sounds with ease and clarity. In assessing an illness, clinicians typically used Occam's razor, named after William of Occam (1285-1349?), an English religious philosopher. Also called the "law of parsimony," it encourages diagnosticians to attribute all the observed phenomena to a single disorder, rather than to several concurrent diseases. Distinctive ailments may coexist, however, and treatment for an illness may produce adverse effects; accordingly, some of the clinical findings may be iatrogenic rather than manifestations of the underlying malady.

Attempting to identify a single disease to explain all the features of an illness, therefore, may be misguided; the limitations and hazards of this approach are encapsulated in the title of an editorial, *Is Occam's Razor Disposable*?[75]
A further problem in analyzing Mozart's death involves the nature of the testimony. The descriptions of his disorder primarily originate from family members who had no medical background and who provided reminiscences only several decades after the event, when faltering memories or a desire to portray the composer in a certain posthumous light may have corrupted their accounts.

Moreover, the absence of any of Mozart's remains that could be examined using modern scientific techniques renders any diagnosis of his fatal illness speculative and unverifiable. All these factors make all suggested diagnoses tentative; peremptory, or even confident, conclusions are unjustified.

As told, Mozart became ill about November 20, 1791, and died 15 days later. During his illness, his physician, Thomas Franz Closset (1754-1813), a renowned practitioner, received assistance from a younger colleague,

---

[75] *Journal of the Royal Society of Medicine*, Volume 80, November 1987, p. 722.

Mathias von Sallaba (1764-1797), who had published several scientific essays and an influential medical text in 1791. Thus, two of Vienna's finest clinicians cared for Mozart, but unfortunately their only direct testimony is the cause of death that Closset recorded in the register of St Stephen's Cathedral on December 5, 1791: "*hitziges Frieselfieber*" [severe miliary fever].

This diagnosis had no more precise meaning then than it has now. Apparently, it indicated fever and a rash, although the latter may have been a nonspecific complication of high temperature, poor hygiene, or profuse sweating, such as miliaria (prickly heat), folliculitis, or transient acantholytic dermatosis (Grover disease).

Obituaries mention "dropsy of the heart" or that Mozart was "dropsical," terms denoting edema. In 1798, Rochlitz's anecdotes, quoted in the "Rumors of Poisoning" section, described fainting episodes while Mozart worked on the Requiem, and Niemetschek's biography, published the same year, asserted, "During his illness Mozart maintained full consciousness right up to his end, and he died at peace, though very unwillingly [...]. The doctors were not agreed about the cause of his death." While visiting Vienna in 1816, a physician, Carl von Bursy, recorded in his diary:

> The most distinguished doctor of the town considered Mozart's illness to be inflammatory and ordered bloodletting. The catarrh developed into a nervous fever, which was prevalent at that time.[76]

In August 1824, during his attempt to exonerate Salieri from the charge of poisoning Mozart, the literatus Giuseppe Carpani solicited a letter from Dr. Eduard Guldener von Lobes, written in Italian. Although Guldener had examined the cadaver, he had not seen Mozart during life. Nevertheless, his colleague, Closset, had apprised him of the patient's condition almost daily, and in his letter Guldener summarized his recollections:

> [...] He fell sick in the late autumn of a rheumatic and inflammatory fever, which being fairly general among us at that time, attacked many people. I did not know about it until a few days later, when his condition had already grown much worse, I did not visit him for some reason, but in-

---

[76] Medical Journal Article: *What Killed Mozart?, op. cit.*.

formed myself of his condition through Dr. Closset, with whom I came in contact almost every day. The latter considered Mozart's illness to be dangerous, and from the very beginning feared a fatal conclusion, namely a deposit on the brain. One day he met Dr. Sallaba and he said positively, "Mozart is lost, it is no longer possible to restrain the deposit". Sallaba communicated this information to me at once, and in fact, Mozart died a few days later with the usual symptoms of a deposit on the brain. His death aroused general interest, but the very slightest suspicion of his having been poisoned entered no one's mind. So many persons saw him during his illness, so many enquired after him, his family tended him with so much care, his doctor, highly regarded by all, the industrious and experienced Closset, treated him with all the attention of a scrupulous physician, and with the interest of a friend of many years' standing, in such a way that certainly it could not have escaped their notice then if even the slightest trace of poisoning had manifested itself. The illness took its accustomed course and had its usual duration; Closset had observed it and recognized it with such accuracy that he had forecast its outcome almost to the hour. This malady attacked at this time a great many of the inhabitants of Vienna, and for not a few of them it had the same fatal conclusion and the same symptoms as in the case of Mozart.[...][77]

To modern clinicians, "deposit on the brain" suggests an intracranial mass. In the 18th century, however, a humoral theory of disease still prevailed, and physicians attributed many diseases to toxic substances that provoked inflammation when present in various tissues, such as the joints, where they produced arthritis, and in the thoracic cavity, where they elicited pain and pleural effusions. In this view, such deposits commonly occurred in the brain during serious febrile illnesses, often causing death.

Some ascribe Mozart's death to malpractice on the part of his physician, Dr. Closset. Sophie Weber, in her 1825 account, makes the implication. Borowitz summarizes:

When Mozart appeared to be sinking, one of his doctors, Dr. Nikolaus Closset, was sent

---

[77] Dobling, 10 June 1824. Cf. OTTO ERICH DEUTSCH, *Mozart. A documentary bibliography*, Stanford, California: Stanford University Press, 1965, p. 523.

for and finally located at the theater. However, according to Sophie's account, that drama-lover "had to wait till the piece was over." When he arrived, he ordered cold compresses put on Mozart's feverish brow, but these "provided such a shock that he did not regain consciousness again before he died.[78]

In 1829, the British musical publisher Vincent Novello (1781-1861) and his wife Mary Sabilla (1789-1854), interviewed Mozart's widow, Constanze, whose second husband, a Danish diplomat named Georg Nissen, had written a biography of Mozart, posthumously published in 1828. Their travel diaries were discovered and published in 1955 and represent an important document because the Novellos were generally reliable. Since they kept separate diaries, their notes can be checked against one another.

In 1825, while preparing his biography, Nissen received a letter from Constanze's sister, Sophie Haibel, who had observed Mozart's death. She recounted some of the events:

---

[78] BOROWITZ ALBERT, *Salieri and the "Murder" of Mozart*, The Musical Quarterly 59 (2), April 1973, pp. 265-266.

Now, when Mozart fell ill, we both made him a night-shirt which he could put on from the front, for he could not turn over because of the swelling . . . . [When she visited him on the day of his death,] he called to me at once, "Ah, dear Sophie, it is good of you to come. You must stay here tonight, you must see me die [...]. I have the taste of death on my tongue already" [...]. [The physician] came and prescribed cold compresses on his burning head, and these gave him such a shock that he did not regain consciousness before he passed away. The last thing he did was to try and mouth the sound of the timpani in his Requiem.[79]

In the biography, Nissen mentioned Sophie's other recollections:

My sister-in-law thinks Mozart was not sufficiently well looked after in his illness, for instead of driving out the fever by other methods, they bled him and applied cold compresses to his head, whereupon his forces visibly forsook him and he lost consciousness, which he never recovered. Even in his serious illness he never became

[79] Medical Journal Article: *What Killed Mozart?, op. cit.*

impatient, and at the end his fine ear and feeling were still sensitive to the song of his pet, a canary, which even had to be removed from the next room, because it overtaxed his emotions.[80]

Nissen also summarized Mozart's quietus:

His final illness, during which he was bedridden, lasted 15 days. It began with swelling in his hands and feet, and an almost complete inability to move: this illness, which later was followed by sudden vomiting, is called a heated miliary fever. He remained fully conscious until two hours before his end.[81]

In his notes, Nissen stated that Constanze reported, "Suddenly, he began to vomit – it spat out of him in an arch, brown and he was dead".[82]

Some have argued that Mozart died of uremia. They cite an earlier illness in 1784 that Mozart's father, Leopold, described in a letter:

My son has been very ill in Vienna. At a performance [...] he perspired so profusely that his clothes were drenched [...]. So not only

---

[80] Idem.

[81] Idem.

[82] Idem.

my son, but a number of other people caught rheumatic fever, which became septic when not taken in hand at once. My son writes as follows, "Four days running at the very same hour I had a violent attack of colic, which ended each time in violent vomiting."[83]

Interpretations include kidney stones and urinary tract infection, with permanent damage producing chronic renal disease. In these theories, Sophie's report of "a great pain in his loins and a general languour spreading over him in degrees" indicates a recurrent attack, and a progressive, fatal decline over the next several months ensued, with the "taste of death" on his tongue being a symptom of uremia. Moreover, although chronic renal failure could explain edema without dyspnea and has a substantial mortality rate, it is not an epidemic disorder associated with fever, rash, limb inflammation, and preserved mentation.

Another proposed diagnosis, citing much of the same evidence, is *Henoch-Schönlein purpura* (HSP), named after two German physi-

---

[83] Idem.

cians who described some of this disease's features in the 19th century.

Most common in children and often preceded by an upper respiratory tract infection, it is an immune complex disease with IgA[84] deposits occurring primarily in the alimentary tract, kidneys, joints, and skin. Its major gastrointestinal manifestations are abdominal pain, diarrhea, and bloody stools. It causes a glomerulonephritis that results in hematuria, proteinuria, and, sometimes, renal failure. The salient rheumatologic finding is self-limited arthralgias, and the cutaneous hallmark is palpable purpura, predominantly on the lower extremities and buttocks. Studies of large numbers of patients suggest that the clinical diagnosis rests on fulfilling most of these criteria: *a.* palpable purpura, *b.* bowel angina, *c.* gastrointestinal bleeding, *d.* hematuria, and *e.* age of onset younger than 21 years. Its appearance in a 35-year-old man like Mozart would be unusual, but possible.

---

[84] IgA nephropathy (also known as IgA nephritis, IgAN, Berger's disease, Berger's syndrome and synpharyngitic glomerulonephritis) is a form of glomerulonephritis (*i.e.* inflammation of the glomeruli of the kidney. This disease was also called "Wassersucht" in Austria).

Series 30-32 of adult patients reported in the 1980s and 1990s indicate that fever occurs in about 10% to 20%, arthralgias in 70%, renal involvement in 60% to 70%, renal insufficiency in 10%, gastrointestinal symptoms in 60%, and relapses in 35%. Acute or chronic renal failure is uncommon, and death is rare. Although *Henoch-Schönlein purpura* could explain certain features of Mozart's illness, epidemics do not occur, the mortality rate of its acute stage is insubstantial, and altered mentation would have been likely if uremia caused his death.

A further diagnosis is acute rheumatic fever. When first used, the term rheumatism (which originates from the Greek *rheumatismos*, meaning "a flowing down") referred to the idea of a liquid humor dripping into a joint to cause inflammation. In its several verbal variations, including "acute rheumatic fever," it remained a nonspecific diagnosis for problems in diverse locations, commonly the joints, but also elsewhere, as indicated in Leopold Mozart's letter in 1784, in which he described his son as suffering from "acute rheumatic fever" when the symptoms were vomiting and colic. Similarly, Wolfgang wrote in 1790: "my head is covered with bandages due to rheumatic pains". The recognition that what is now called "acute rheumatic fever" had extra-articular manifestations came slowly.

Although Thomas Sydenham (1624-1689) described chorea in 1686, only in the late 18th and early 19th centuries did clinicians recognize its association with acute rheumatism. Similarly, widespread appreciation that heart damage could accompany rheumatic disease finally emerged in the early 1800s, partly from the reports of William Charles Wells (1757-1823), who also described subcutaneous nodules in 1812 and mentioned erythema, although not definitively erythema marginatum, in 1810. In the Harvey Lectures published in 1889, Walter Cheadle (1836-1910) provided the first comprehensive view of the clinical manifestations of acute rheumatic fever, as they are currently understood. This historical information demonstrates that Guldener's description of Mozart's illness as "a rheumatic and inflammatory fever" does not necessarily correspond to what is now called "acute rheumatic fever" an immunologic reaction to a pharyngeal infection with Streptococcus pyogenes (group A streptococcus) that can affect the heart, joints, skin, and central nervous system. Those supporting this diagnosis as Mozart's fatal illness suggest that two earlier episodes occurred in childhood. In November 1766, his father, Leopold, wrote a letter describing how his son had been sick at age seven in January 1763:

> Little Wolfgang fell ill and was very sick [...] finally the trouble settled in his feet, where he complained of pains and so forth. Now he has a similar attack. He could not stand on his feet or move his toes or knees. No one could come near him and for four nights he could not sleep [...]. The whole time, and especially towards evening, he was very hot and feverish. Today he is noticeably better; but it will certainly be a week before he is quite restored to health.

Acute rheumatic fever and other diseases, such as rheumatoid arthritis and viral infections, are plausible diagnoses. If these illnesses were indeed attacks of acute rheumatic fever, however, they left no apparent permanent *sequelae*, for Mozart was physically vigorous throughout his adult life.

The clinical diagnosis of acute rheumatic fever currently rests on criteria first proposed by T. Duckett Jones in 1944, subsequently revised several times. The latest version requires the presence of two major or one major and two minor criteria, conjoined with evidence of a preceding group A streptococcal infection. The major criteria are carditis, polyarthritis, chorea, subcutaneous nodules, and erythema marginatum. The minor criteria include a history of previous rheumatic fever or rheumatic heart disease, arthralgia, fever, and abnormal results of tests unavailable in Mozart's time: an increased erythrocyte sedimentation rate or C-reactive protein and a prolonged PR interval on electrocardiogram. The information about Mozart's fatal illness cannot satisfy Jones' criteria, but does permit an analysis of whether his disease corresponds to the clinical features of acute rheumatic fever. That disorder can cause fever and a rash, erythema marginatum, which is a serpiginous macular eruption, often evanescent and typically found on the trunk and proximal extremities. It almost never occurs in adults, however. Acute rheumatic fever produces inflammation of the extremities. The polyarthritis generally affects the large joints in a sequential manner, as a migratory phenomenon (inflammation resolves in one joint before appearing in another) or as an "additive" one (inflammation afflicts a new joint while remaining in a previously affected one). Involvement of the joints of the hands and feet, described in Mozart, however, is uncommon. Acute rheumatic fever can cause edema when heart failure occurs from valvular disease, primarily mitral regurgitation but also aortic regurgitation or mitral stenosis. Pericarditis can develop, rarely producing cardiac tamponade and peripheral edema. With either cardiac disorder, however, dyspnea occurs, and no account of Mozart's illness mentions it.

In fatal acute rheumatic fever, mentation preserved until death is certainly expected. Acute rheumatic fever is an epidemic disease, but without an organized reporting system in Mozart's time, clinicians may not have recognized outbreaks unless they affected large numbers. Such circumstances certainly exist: in the congested barracks during World War II, US recruits had a peak incidence of acute rheumatic fever exceeding 10%. Possibly, its frequency attained such levels in Vienna.

The acute disease, however, does not have a substantial mortality rate. Death generally occurs from chronic valvular damage that becomes clinically apparent years to decades after the original episodes. In acute attacks, the earliest mortality rates recorded, from the middle to late 19th century, were only 1% to

5%, even among those ill enough to require hospitalization. Acute rheumatic fever, therefore, fails to explain several features of Mozart's illness. Moreover, it has always been primarily a childhood disorder, with adults uncommonly affected. Even in those who had attacks as children, recurrent episodes during adulthood are unusual, especially in somebody 35 years old, and acute rheumatic fever uncommonly involves the heart in adults: arthritis is typically the preeminent manifestation. Furthermore, the rheumatologic and cardiac components are usually inversely related: the disease "licks the joints and bites the heart" or "bites the joints and licks the heart". If acute rheumatic fever caused Mozart's inflamed extremities, cardiac involvement would likely have been minimal or absent. In addition, attacks of acute rheumatic fever tend to be mimetic, each episode affecting the same sites as previous ones. Mozart's two suspicious childhood illnesses consisted primarily of joint complaints, but no cardiac symptoms, such as pain from pericarditis or dyspnea from significant valvular damage, suggesting that a subsequent episode during adulthood should also have included no heart complications. Certainly, he might have had subclinical valve damage detectable only with auscultation, a technique unavailable then. Those who died of acute rheumatic fever, however, usually already had severe heart disease, something that Mozart's previous physical vigor discounts.

Another hypothesis is that his fatal illness was infective endocarditis, which might explain the fever and the skin lesions, which include petechiae, Osler nodes, and Janeway lesions. It would account for the inflamed extremities (arthritic and musculoskeletal complaints are common); mentation is typically preserved until death; and it was a lethal disease. When edema occurs, however, its origin is almost always heart failure caused by valvular damage, and dyspnea is present. Conceivably, glomerulonephritis associated with bacterial endocarditis could have caused edema without dyspnea, but it uncommonly causes the nephrotic syndrome. Finally, infective endocarditis is not an epidemic disease.

In 1829 interview by the Novellos, Constanze said that Mozart suspected foul play:

> [...] I know I must die, [...] someone has given me acqua toffana and has calculated the precise time of my death for which they

have ordered a Requiem, it is for myself I am writing this.[85]

Sophie added that Mozart's "arms and limbs were much inflamed and swollen."[86] Sophie recalled phlebotomies, and von Bursy's diary also indicated that the physician ordered bloodletting. Because Mozart was a small man, 163 cm (5 ft 4 in) tall, and venesections then were often voluminous, they may have accelerated, or even caused, his demise.

Acqua toffana, originally formulated by a Neopolitan woman, Tofana, was a colorless and tasteless liquid containing arsenic, sold ostensibly as a cosmetic to Italian women in the 17th century, with the claim that it was a miraculous substance oozing from the tomb of St. Nicholas di Bari; a saint of healing. In truth, many used it as a poison – especially young women who wished to hasten the arrival of widowhood. In her interview with the Novellos, however, Constanze dismissed Mozart's fear of poisoning as "an absurd idea," and her husband's biography of Mozart had attempted to refute this rumor.

---

[85] Medical Journal Article: *What Killed Mozart?, op. cit.*.

[86] Idem.

The conspiracy theories, devoid of historical merit, also lack medical credibility. The clinical features of acute arsenic poisoning that observers should have recorded include throat burning, dysphagia, abdominal pain, nausea, vomiting, and diarrhea. Other prominent findings are hypotension, cyanosis, dyspnea, delirium, coma, and seizures. With chronic arsenic poisoning, the major manifestations are a sensorimotor polyneuropathy, an erythroderma, and respiratory complaints related to tracheitis, bronchitis, and laryngitis.

Another poisoning theory is that Mozart accidentally died from miscalculating the dose while treating himself for syphilis with mercury the clinical course summarized by an aphorism attributed to a US physician, J. Earle Moore (1892-1957), "two minutes with Venus, two years with mercury." No credible evidence supports the diagnosis of syphilis, and accounts of his demise do not mention the typical, prominent features of mercury poisoning: memory loss, excessive salivation, and erethism (from the Greek, meaning "irritation"), which denotes emotional lability, irritability, forgetfulness, timidity, and delirium. Inspection of his handwriting shows no evidence of intention tremor, probably the most common manifestation of chronic mercury poisoning.

In a journal article dated 1908, it was suggested that Vitamin D deficiency could have played a role in Mozart's underlying medical conditions leading to his death.[87] If only Mozart had spent a little more time outdoors enjoying the sunshine – because then we might have had a few more masterpieces. Scientists discovered the composer, who died at just 35, did not get enough sunlight. He lived in Austria, which was darker than most of Europe, and would work through the night and sleep during the day. This prevented his body from producing sufficient levels of vitamin D. The 'sunshine vitamin' is essential for bone health and is produced when the skin is exposed to the ultraviolet B sunrays.

Vitamin D deficiency is linked to many medical conditions, and increases the risk of developing influenza, pneumonia, certain cancers, cardiovascular disease and musculoskeletal pain.

A 1994 article in Neurology suggests Mozart died from a fractured skull that had led to a

---

[87] GRANT W.B. - PILS S., *Vitamin D deficiency contributed to Mozart's death*, Medical Problems of Performing Artists, 26 N2, 117, 2011.

chronic subdural hematoma.[88] What is the evidence for this suggestion? Pierre-Francoise Puech, a French anthropologist of the University of Provence, claimed to have studied the purported skull of Mozart and sighted a fracture that he attributed to the many falls Mozart sustained in 1791.[89] Puech claims that chronic bruising put Mozart in a coma and killed him, which could explain Mozart's depression and dizziness right before his death. The skull was supposed to have been rescued by a gravedigger named Joseph Rothmayer during the reorganization of the composer's grave, who later passed on/gave it to anatomist Josef Hyrtl, the municipality of Salzburg, and the Mozarteum museum (Salzburg). Three years later, the American physician, Niles E. Drake, concurred with Puech's theory in an article that was published in the journal *BioScience*. This theory would indeed help explain why Mozart was depressed and dizzy not long before his death. The obvious problem with this theory is that there is still no consensus as

---

[88] DRAKE JR, *Mozart's chronic subdural hematoma*, Neurology 43 (11): 2400–3, ME, 1993.

[89] The skull of W.A. Mozart was exhumed in 1801 at the cemetery in Vienna, Austria (*La Chronique Medicale*, 13, 1906).

to whether the skull actually belonged to Mozart. Rothmayer had allegedly wrapped wire
around the neck of Mozart's corpse before
burying it, and had retrieved the skull ten
years later when it was exhumed. Research
had concluded that the skull belonged to a 20-
40-year-old South German male who suffered
a developmental abnormality called prema-
ture synopsis of the metopic suture (PSMS).
This abnormality is characterised by the bone
of the forehead developing in two halves, and
the failure of the metopic suture to close after
birth, resulting in a broad midface and a small,
abnormally-shaped skull. As Mozart's portraits
depicted a straight, vertical forehead, bulbous
nose, prominent cheekbones and upper lip,
and prominent brow arches, it was supposed
that the skull did indeed belong to him. Further research involving the superimposition of
a photograph of the cranium of the skull on
portraits of Mozart painted between 1778 and
1788 indicated conformity with all side proportions of the head.

However, Nova Scotian neurologist Professor
TJ Murray, who founded the Dalhousie Society
for the History of Medicine, denied that the
skull was that of Mozart as seen in portraits.
Walter Brauneis, archivist of the Office for the

Preservation of Historical Monuments in Austria, undertook to carry out his own research by locating official medical records concerning Mozart's death. Surprisingly he found a doctor's description of the body, which noted that Mozart had only seven teeth remaining in his mouth (the rest having rotted or fallen out!) When the Mozarteum skull was re-examined, it was found to have four more teeth than had been recorded by the doctor. Puech supporters countered that the doctor probably counted only the healthy teeth.

The only way to be sure just whose skull it is would be to perform DNA analysis on the skull; unfortunately, all of Mozart's children died childless, and it would be unwise to disturb his parents' grave.

Another hypothesis is based on trichinosis. In 2001 speculations upon the nature of the disease that killed Mozart took an abrupt turn when infectious disease specialist Dr. Jan V Hirschmann argued that Mozart's death was caused by – pork chops. Hirschmann, of Puget Sound Veterans Affairs Medical Center and the University of Washington in Seattle, who discussed this subject in the journal Archives of Internal Medicine, pointed out what he believed to be a significant clue in a letter dated 7-8 October, 1791 from Mozart to his wife:

> [...] What do I smell? Why, here is Don Primus with the pork cutlets! Che gusto! Now I am eating to your health! It is striking eleven o'clock [...].

Mozart's favourite food had always been pork. In this case, it may have been his favourite pork chops that killed him – or rather, what was in them. The plausibility of this diagnosis, however, depends on Mozart's diet: it requires evidence that he ate meat, especially pork.

The disease trichinosis, caused by a parasitic worm called *Trichinella* and spread by improperly-cooked tainted meat, was not discovered until 1860[90] when a woman who died of a mysterious disease with symptoms similar to Mozart's – fever, weakness, anorexia, con-

---

[90] James Paget, a 21-year-old, first-year medical student attending an autopsy of a patient who died of tuberculosis at St Bartholomew's Hospital in London, in 1825 observed a large number of cysts containing worms; however, the connection between the worms and disease was not made until 35 years later.

stipation and excruciating muscle pain – was found to harbour a large number of wriggling worms in her muscles. When the pathologist, Friedrich von Zenker (1825-1898), discovered that others at the inn where she worked had developed a similar disease (including a butcher who had prepared the meat for a Christmas meal she had attended), he set about examining the ham and sausage from a pig slaughtered for the festivities – and found the same worms in the muscle tissue. When Zenker fed the tainted meat to animals, he found worms in their alimentary canal.

The incubation period for trichinosis is usually between eight and 15 days, although it can take up to 50 days for the worms to start wreaking havoc. Liberated from their cysts by the digestive juices in the host's stomach, the larvae travel to the small intestine and invade the columnar epithelium layer where they moult four times before maturing. Five days after mating, the females give birth to live larvae, which penetrate the intestinal wall, enter the lymphatic system, and move via the bloodstream to areas of implantation – namely, tissue, although they can only survive in skeletal muscle where they form cysts. Typical symptoms include muscle and joint pain, high fever, weakness, nausea and vomiting, diarrhoea, swelling of the face, headache, fatigue and generalised swelling due to the leakage of fluid from damaged vessels into surrounding tissue – all of which echo Mozart's symptoms in his final throes of disease. The patient typically has preserved mentation, although in the final stages of the disease may develop strokes, seizures, encephalitis and coma, and death usually occurs within the second or third week of the disease from pneumonia or from neurological or cardiac complications. Fatal trichinosis is now rare, but shortly after the first clinical description in 1860, reports of German epidemics appeared, detailing varying, but sometimes substantial, mortality rates. In 1863, for example, 153 cases, 18% of which were lethal, occurred in Hettstädt following pork consumption at festivities celebrating the 50th anniversary of the Battle of Leipzig.

In 1865, 337 people became ill in Hedersleden, with a 30% fatality rate, and a retrospective analysis of an outbreak in Wegeleben in 1849 revealed 160 cases, 19% of which were lethal. Trichinosis, then, could explain all the features of Mozart's disease.

The only problem with this theory of course is that, while it explains virtually all of Mozart's symptoms, it does not quite follow the progression of Mozart's disease, assuming that the testimonies of his witness can be relied upon. The earlier stage of the disease should have been largely asymptomatic, but accompanied by diarrhoea and abdominal pain as the worms lodged themselves in the intestine, it was only when the immune system geared up against the invaders that the rash, swelling and pain should have begun.

Furthermore, despite Hirschmann's contention that no shortness of breath had been observed, it is highly unlikely that a cardioneurological disorder that caused Mozart's death would not be associated with respiratory difficulty. A medical practitioner who was consulted regarding this matter confirmed that the arrhythmia would have brought about fluctuations in blood pressure and consequently in the amount of oxygen transported as well, not to mention disturbances in the bloodstream's electrolyte balance. In any event, it is inconceivable that anyone should die of pneumonia or heart complications without suffering breathing problems!

Other suspected diseases to explain Mozart's death at an early age include hypochondria, cerebral hemorrhage, abuse of medicines containing antimony to relieve the fever he suffered, or stroke, and typhus fever.

Modern scholars have tossed aside the popular yet unconvincing theory that Mozart was poisoned, and are focusing on a more plausible cause of death, sickness. He was simply exhausted! It has been established that Mozart suffered from various illnesses, which no doubt contributed to his death. But some researchers have concluded that physical and mental exhaustion greatly affected Mozart, and contributed to his early death.

Mozart's father himself described in a letter his son's precarious health state: rheumatic fever in 1766 and 1784 (as previously stated), smallpox in 1767, severe frostbite in 1770, hepatitis in 1771, a painful dental abscess in 1774, bronchitis in 1780 and a serious streptococcal infection in 1787.

These researchers claim that by cramming more work and play into one year than most people did in ten years, Mozart literally "burned himself out". The constant strain on his body forced it to succumb to the plaguing illnesses that continuously nagged at Mozart's health, and that he otherwise might have been able to withstand. It has been said that Mozart had a peculiar mental and physical lifestyle, and that he was a child who never grew up. Physically, he had childlike energy levels, and worked at an incredibly exhausting pace. The only way he knew to gain respect was to write music. An early Mozart biographer, Ignaz Arnold wrote, "No need for poison here – his powers were worn out, his constitution destroyed". He also wrote "what straining of his imagination, what constant wearing-down of his spirit, what excitement of his brain fibers! What continuous sapping of his vital life forces!" In a word: his whole life was – the consumption of life. History shows us a host of great spirits who burned themselves out. In this passage, he is talking about the destruction of Mozart's "creative energies". He also wrote about Mozart's physical exhaustion in his last few months of life: two operas (*La Clemenza di Tito* and *Die Zauberflöte*), a clarinet concerto, two cantatas, the incomplete *Requiem*, six piano concertos, one piano quintet, one string quartet, and two sonatas and two sets of variations for piano as well as a few smaller compositions. This enormous output was not the work of a composer writing in undisturbed peace and seclusion, but of one whose schedule included teaching obligations, as well as all kinds of other distractions of which would have been enough to make an ordinary person nervous. And all of this is more amazing considering that Mozart was sickly and frail. Despite these setbacks, he almost never slowed his pace. For years, often during sickness, Mozart continued to compose, give performances, travel, teach, and maintain a lively social life. It is clear that Mozart was always on the go, and this could not have been healthy for him, considering his physical state. I believe that his grueling schedule led to exhaustion, which, along with his illness, finally led to his death.

Mozart was a frail man, and continuous bouts with different diseases led him to become increasingly unhealthy. The people who are trying to piece together what disease killed Mozart believe that whichever disease it was, he probably suffered from it previously.

After more than 250 years, however, it is difficult to assess the real cause of Mozart's death: a lot of hypothesis, guesswork, theories. His demise is wrapped in the shadow, in a mysterious aura, the same that characterised and will always feature his life and works.

MOZART AND NUMBERS

The keywords of this chapter are 'Fibonacci sequence' and 'Golden mean'; the principles are closely related.[91] While the exact relationship between music and mathematics is still under debate, the present investigation sets out to describe Mozart's music mathematically. This structural analysis of the music and its effects on the listener includes examples of the application of mathematics to music, the measurement of the effects of Mozart's music, the application of the golden ratio to Mozart's musical structure, and an analysis of the application of mathematics to the musical structure of Mozart concerts. These analyses strongly suggest the close correlation between music and mathematics.

Let's get started from the basics of this research. Fibonacci – whom the sequence at issue is called after –[92] was known in his time and is still recognized today as the "greatest

---

[91] Other possible names are: Golden ratio, Phi, Divine Section, Golden Cut, Golden Proportion, Divine Proportion, Golden number and Tau(t).

[92] The name "Fibonacci sequence" was first used by the 19th-century number theorist Édouard Lucas.

European mathematician of the middle ages." He was born in the 1170s and died in the 1240s and there is now a statue commemorating him located at the Leaning Tower end of the cemetery next to the Cathedral in Pisa. Fibonacci's name is also perpetuated in two streets the quayside Lungarno Fibonacci in Pisa and the Via Fibonacci in Florence.

His full name was Leonardo of Pisa, or Leonardo Pisano in Italian since he was born in Pisa, Tuscany. He called himself Fibonacci which was short for Filius Bonacci, standing for "son of Bonacci", which was his father's name. Leonardo's father, Guglielmo Bonacci, was a kind of customs officer in the North African town of Bugia, now called Bougie. So Fibonacci grew up with a North African education under the Moors and later travelled extensively around the Mediterranean coast. He then met with many merchants and learned of their systems of doing arithmetic. He soon realized the many advantages of the "Hindu-Arabic" system over all the others. He was one of the first people to introduce the Hindu-Arabic number system into Europe – the system we now use today – based of ten digits with its decimal point and a symbol for zero: 1 2 3 4 5 6 7 8 9 and 0.

His book on how to do arithmetic in the decimal system, called *Liber abbaci* (meaning Book of the Abacus or Book of calculating) completed in 1202 persuaded many of the European mathematicians of his day to use his "new" system. The book, written in Latin, goes into detail with the rules we all now learn in elementary school for adding, subtracting, multiplying and dividing numbers altogether with many problems to illustrate the methods in detail.

The root of Fibonacci sequence is associated to the growth of an idealized (biologically unrealistic) rabbit population. Indeed, the mathematician assuming that: a newly born pair of rabbits, one male, one female, are put in a field; rabbits are able to mate at the age of one month so that at the end of its second month a female can produce another pair of rabbits; rabbits never die and a mating pair always produces one new pair (one male, one female) every month from the second month on. The puzzle that Fibonacci posed was: how many pairs will there be in one year?

- ✓ At the end of the first month, they mate, but there is still only 1 pair;

- ✓ At the end of the second month the female produces a new pair, so now there are 2 pairs of rabbits in the field;
- ✓ At the end of the third month, the original female produces a second pair, making 3 pairs in all in the field;
- ✓ At the end of the fourth month, the original female has produced yet another new pair, the female born two months ago produces her first pair also, making 5 pairs;

And so forth...

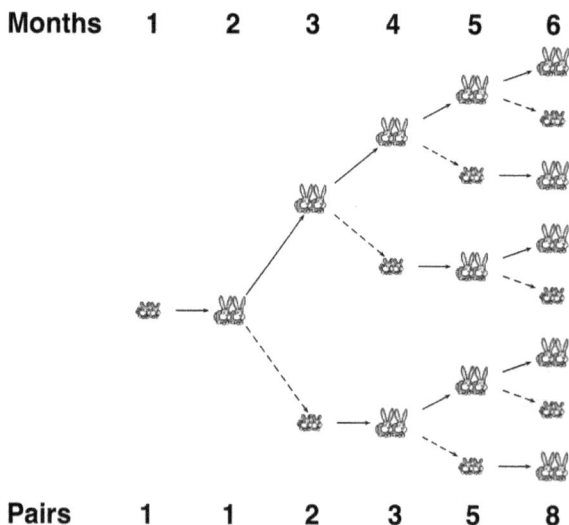

Months	1	2	3	4	5	6
Pairs	1	1	2	3	5	8

Then, from month to month, the number of rabbit couples will be:

MONTH	MONTH NO.	CALCULATION	RABBIT COUPLES
JANUARY	1	1 + 0 =	1
FEBRUARY	2	1 + 0 =	1
MARCH	3	1 + 1 =	2
APRIL	4	2 + 1 =	3
MAY	5	3 + 2 =	5
JUNE	6	5 + 3 =	8
JULY	7	8 + 5 =	13
AUGUST	8	13 + 8 =	21
SEPTEMBER	9	21 + 13=	34
OCTOBER	10	34 + 21=	55
NOVEMBER	11	55 + 34=	89
DECEMBER	12	89 + 55=	144

For any month's total number of rabbits, you add the number of rabbits existing one month earlier to the number of rabbits born since then – the same as the number of rabbits existing two months earlier.

Generalizing this to a mathematical formula, we can say that:

$$x_N = x_{N-1} + x_{N-2} \, (x_0 = 1, x_1 = 1)$$

where:

- ✓ x represents the number of rabbit couples;
- ✓ n represents the number of the month, 0, 1, 2 etc., and so forth;

✓ *xn* is the number of rabbits existing in month *n*;

This sequence is constructed by choosing arbitrarily the first two numbers (the "seeds" of the sequence) then assigning the rest by the rule that each number be the sum of the two preceding numbers. This simple rule generates a sequence of numbers having many surprising properties, of which scholars focus their attention on a few:

✓ Take any three adjacent numbers in the sequence, square the middle number, and multiply the first and third numbers. The difference between these two results is always 1;
✓ Take any four adjacent numbers in the sequence. Multiply the outside ones. Multiply the inside ones. The first product will be either one more or one less than the second;
✓ The sum of any ten adjacent numbers equals 11 times the seventh one of the ten.

The Fibonacci sequence is but one example of many sequences with simple recursion relations.

The Fibonacci sequence obeys the recursion relation $P(N) = P(N-1) + P(N-2)$. Dividing each number in the series by the one that precedes it produces a ratio which converges to a value of 1.618033988..., called "phi", whose symbol is ϕ or φ. Sometimes the Greek letter "tau", τ, is used.

A striking feature of this sequence is that the reciprocal of ϕ is 0.6180339887..., which is ϕ - 1. Put another way, $\phi = 1/\phi + 1$. This is true whatever two seed integers you use to start the sequence, this result depends only on the recursion relation you use, not the choice of seeds. Therefore, there are many different sequences that converge to ϕ. They are called "generalized Fibonacci sequences".

The ratio ϕ = 1.6180339887... is called the "golden ratio". A rectangle that has sides in this proportion is called the "golden rectangle", and it was known to the ancient Greeks. The golden rectangle is the basis for generating a curve known as the "golden spiral", a logarithmic spiral that is fairly well-matched to some spirals found in nature, and this fact is

the source of much of the popular and mystical interest in this mathematical subject.

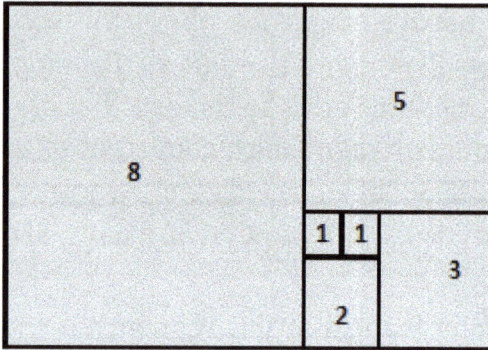

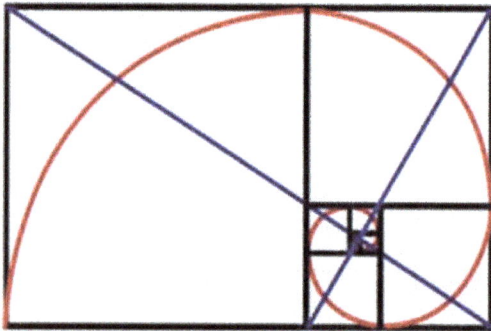

Writers on this subject sometimes concen-
trate on ϕ and some on $1/\phi$ as the ratio of interest. This is no "big deal" for when we have
a ratio of two values, say A and B, which is a
comparison of their sizes, the reciprocal of the
ratio A to B is just the ratio of B to A.

This theory dates back at the time of Plato, a Greek philosopher theorized. He believed that if a line was divided into two unequal segments so that the smaller segment was related to the larger in the same way that the larger segment was related to the whole, what would result would be a special proportional relationship. That is what he meant by Golden mean:

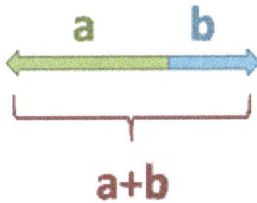

We will have this formula:

a+b is to *a* as *a* is to *b*

We can continue adding squares around the first picture, each new square having a side which is as long as the sum of the latest two square's sides. This set of rectangles whose sides are two successive Fibonacci numbers in length and which are composed of squares with sides which are Fibonacci numbers, is called the Fibonacci Rectangles.

The second diagram shows that we can draw a spiral by putting together quarter circles, one in each new square. This is a spiral (the Fibonacci Spiral). A similar curve to this occurs in nature as the shape of a snail shell or some sea shells. Whereas the Fibonacci Rectangles spiral increases in size by a factor of Phi (1.618...) in a quarter of a turn (*i.e.* a point a further quarter of a turn round the curve is 1.618... times as far from the centre, and this applies to all points on the curve), the Nautilus spiral curve takes a whole turn before points move a factor of 1.618... from the centre.

The Fibonacci sequence is seen in nature, in the arrangement of leaves on a stem of plants, in the pattern of sunflower seeds, spirals of snail's shells, in the number of petals of flowers, in the periods of planets of the solar system, and even in stock market cycles. So pervasive is the sequence in nature (according to these folks) that one begins to suspect that the series has the remarkable ability to be "fit" to most anything! Nature's processes are "governed" by the golden ratio. Some sources even say that nature's processes are "explained" by this ratio.

Of course much of this is patently nonsense. Mathematics doesn't "explain" anything in nature, but mathematical models are very powerful for describing patterns and laws found in nature. I think it's safe to say that the Fibonacci sequence, golden mean, and golden rectangle have never, not even once, directly led to the discovery of a fundamental law of nature. When we see a neat numeric or geometric pattern in nature, we realize we must dig deeper to find the underlying reason why these patterns arise.

Why is it that the number of petals in a flower is often one of the following numbers: 3, 5, 8, 13, 21, 34 or 55? For example, the lily has three petals, buttercups have five of them, the chicory has 21 of them, the daisy has often 34 or 55 petals, etc. Furthermore, when one observes the heads of sunflowers, one notices two series of curves, one winding in one sense and one in another; the number of spirals not being the same in each sense. Why is the number of spirals, in general, either 21 and 34, either 34 and 55, either 55 and 89, or 89 and 144? The same for pinecones: why do they have either 8 spirals from one side and 13 from the other, or either 5 spirals from one side and 8 from the other? Finally, why is the number of diagonals of a pineapple also 8 in one direction and 13 in the other? Are these numbers the product of chance? No! They all belong to the Fibonacci sequence: 1, 2, 3, 5, 8, 13, 21, 34, 55, 89, 144, etc. (where each number is obtained from the sum of the two preceding). A more abstract way of putting it is that the Fibonacci numbers fn are given by the formula $f1 = 1$, $f2 = 2$, $f3 = 3$, $f4 = 5$, and generally $f_{n+2} = f_{n+1} + f_n$. For a long time, it had been noticed that these numbers were important in nature, but only relatively recently that one understands why. It is a question of efficiency during the growth process of plants.

The explanation is linked to another famous number, the Golden mean, itself intimately linked to the spiral form of certain types of shell. Let's mention also that in the case of the sunflower, the pineapple and of the pinecone, the correspondence with the Fibonacci numbers is very exact, while in the case of the number of flower petals, it is only verified on average (and in certain cases, the number is doubled since the petals are arranged on two levels).

Knowledge of the golden section, ratio and rectangle goes back to the Greeks, who based their most famous work of art on them: the Parthenon is full of golden rectangles. The Greek followers of the mathematician and mystic Pythagoras even thought of the golden ratio as divine.

Later, Leonardo da Vinci painted Mona Lisa's face to fit perfectly into a golden rectangle, and structured the rest of the painting around similar rectangles.

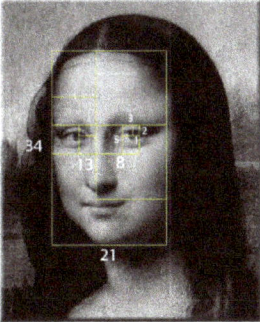

Consistence of Fibonacci structure is even observed in human body. Indeed, every human has two hands, each one of these has five fingers; each finger has three parts which are separated by two knuckles. All of these numbers fit into the sequence.

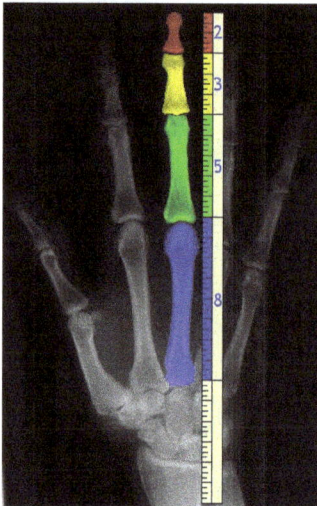

When conducting their researches or setting out their products, artists, scientists and designers take the human body – the proportions of which are set out according to the golden ratio – as their measure. Leonardo da Vinci and Le Corbusier took the human body, proportioned according to the golden ratio, as their measure when producing their designs. The human body, proportioned according to the golden ratio, is taken as the basis also in the Neufert, one of the most important reference books of modern-day architects.

The "ideal" proportional relations that are suggested as existing among various parts of the average human body and that approximately meet the golden ratio values can be set out in a general plan as follows:

The M/m level in the table below is always equivalent to the golden ratio. M/m = 1.618

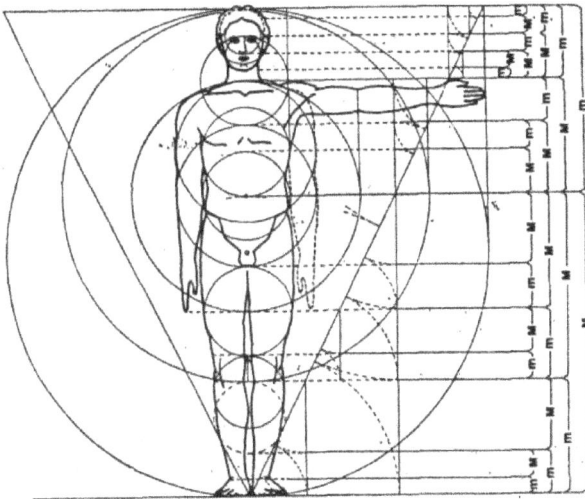

The first example of the golden ratio in the average human body is that when the distance between the navel and the foot is taken as 1 unit, the height of a human being is equivalent to 1.618. Some other golden proportions in the average human body are:

- ✓ The distance between the finger tip and the elbow/distance between the wrist and the elbow;
- ✓ The distance between the shoulder line and the top of the head/head length;
- ✓ The distance between the navel and the top of the head/the distance between the shoulder line and the top of the head;
- ✓ The distance between the navel and knee/distance between the knee and the end of the foot;

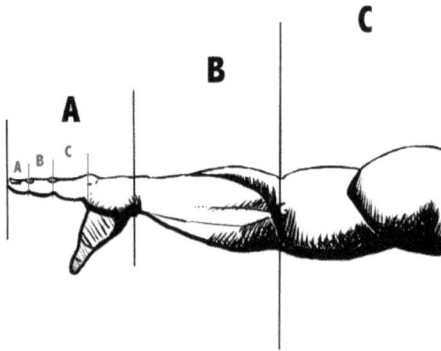

As for the the human hand, one will in all likelihood witness a golden proportion there.

Our fingers have three sections. The proportion of the first two to the full length of the finger gives the golden ratio (with the exception of the thumbs). You can also see that the proportion of the middle finger to the little finger is also a golden ratio.

You have two hands, and the fingers on them consist of three sections. There are five fingers on each hand, and only eight of these are articulated according to the golden number: 2, 3, 5, and 8 fit the Fibonacci numbers.

As for the human face, there are several golden ratios in it. This refers to the "ideal human face" determined by scientists and artists.

For example, the total width of the two front teeth in the upper jaw over their height gives a golden ratio. The width of the first tooth from the centre to the second tooth also yields a golden ratio. These are the ideal proportions that a dentist may consider. Some other golden ratios in the human face are:

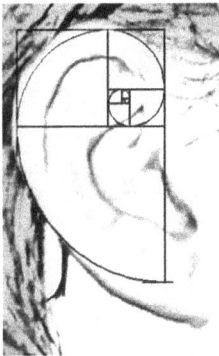

✓ Length of face/width of face;
✓ Distance between the lips and where the eyebrows meet/length of nose;

- ✓ Length of face/distance between tip of jaw and where the eyebrows meet;
- ✓ Length of mouth/width of nose;
- ✓ Width of nose/distance between nostrils;
- ✓ Distance between pupils /distance between eyebrows;

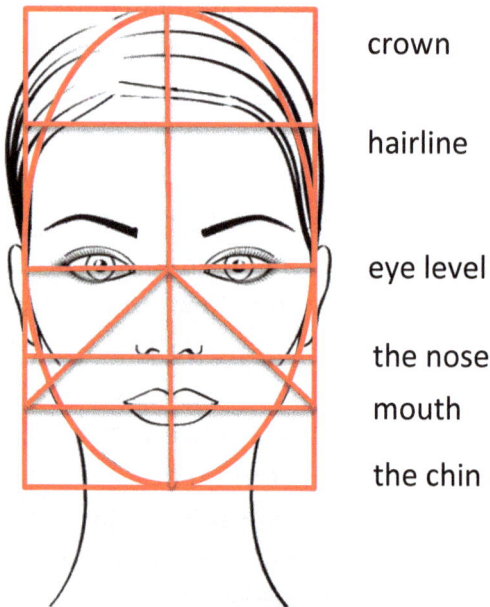

crown

hairline

eye level

the nose

mouth

the chin

After this general overview, introducing the main features of Fibonacci sequence and Golden mean, let's now observe the application of this structure to music and, in particular, to Mozart's.

The relationship between music and mathematics has fascinated generations, and it is generally believed that there is a mystic connection between the two, and that there is some kind of intrinsic affinity between music and mathematics. It is well known how much the Greeks were obsessed with numbers. The Greeks believed that the numbers have some divine values and that there are some numbers which are more perfect than others, and that the universe is governed by numbers. Even the astronomer Galileo observed in 1623 that the entire universe "is written in the language of mathematics". It is indeed remarkable the extent to which science and society are governed by mathematical ideas. From ancient Greek times, music has been seen as a mathematical art. Music, with all its passion and emotion, is also based upon mathematical relationships, and such musical notions as octaves, chords, scales, and keys can all be demystified and understood logically using simple mathematics. There is even a theory which is attributed to Pythagoras that musical notes having simple relative frequencies are necessarily aesthetically preferable to those having complex ones. This theory in fact explains the relationship between mathematics and music, and states that the notes of the musical scale have to be determined by the ratio of a perfect fifth (*i.e.* 3:2. for most aesthetic value).

What Pythagoras had discovered is called the Diatonic musical scale, named after the fact that the string is divided into two lengths (*Dia* = two).

These ratios correspond with the frequencies of the notes produced by the white keys of the piano when attuned in the Diatonic scale. After the 7th note the octave of 8 notes is repeated only this time the first and the eighth note are doubled in frequency! The next 7 notes of the white keys on the piano follow the exact same ratio! Indeed, the word "octave" comes from the Latin word for 8, referring to the eight tones of the complete musical scale.

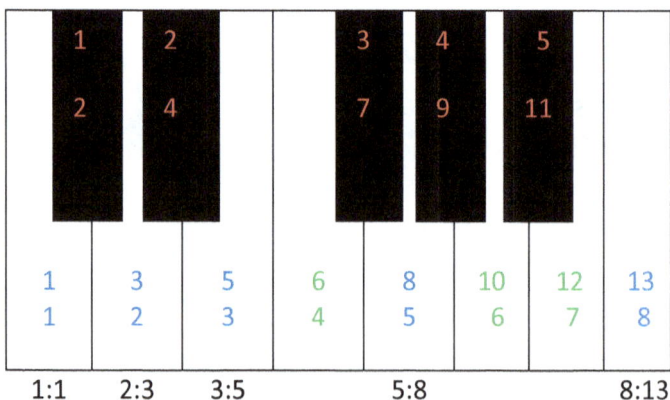

	1 / 2	2 / 4		3 / 7	4 / 9	5 / 11	
1 / 1	3 / 2	5 / 3	6 / 4	8 / 5	10 / 6	12 / 7	13 / 8
1:1	2:3	3:5		5:8			8:13

In a scale, the dominant note is the 5th note of the major scale, which is also the 8th note of all 13 notes that comprise the octave. This provides an added instance of Fibonacci numbers in key musical relationships. Interestingly, 8/13 is .61538, which approximates phi. What's more, the typical three chord song in the key of A is made up of A, its Fibonacci & phi partner E, and D, to which A bears the same relationship as E does to A. This is analogous to the "A is to B as B is to C" basis for the golden section, or in this case "D is to A as A is to E".

Notes in the scale of western music are based on natural harmonics that are created by ratios of frequencies. Ratios found in the first seven numbers of the Fibonacci series (0, 1, 1, 2, 3, 5, 8) are related to key frequencies of musical notes.

Fibonacci Ratio	Calculated Frequency	Tempered Frequency	Note in Scale	Musical Relationship	When A=432 *	Octave Below	Octave Above
1/1	440	440.00	A	Root	432	216	864
2/1	880	880.00	A	Octave	864	432	1728
2/3	293.33	293.66	D	Fourth	288	144	576
2/5	176	174.62	F	Aug Fifth	172.8	86.4	345.6

3/2	660	659.26	E	Fifth	648	324	1296
3/5	264	261.63	C	Minor Third	259.2	129.6	518.4
3/8	165	164.82	E	Fifth	162 (Phi)	81	324
5/2	1,100.00	1,108.72	C#	Third	1080	540	2160
5/3	733.33	740.00	F#	Sixth	720	360	1440
5/8	275	277.18	C#	Third	270	135	540
8/3	1,173.33	1,174.64	D	Fourth	1152	576	2304
8/5	704	698.46	F	Aug. Fifth	691.2	345.6	1382.4

The calculated frequency above starts with A440 and applies the Fibonacci relationships. In practice, pianos are tuned to a "tempered" frequency, a man-made adaptation devised to provide improved tonality when playing in various keys. Pluck a string on a guitar, however, and search for the harmonics by lightly touching the string without making it touch the frets and you will find pure Fibonacci relationships.

A440 is an arbitrary standard. The American Federation of Musicians accepted the A440 as standard pitch in 1917. It was then accepted by the U.S. government its standard in 1920 and it was not until 1939 that this pitch was accepted internationally. Before recent times a variety of tunings were used. It has been suggested by James Furia and others that A432 be the standard. A432 was often used by classical composers and results in a tuning of the whole number frequencies that are connected to numbers used in the construction of a variety of ancient works and sacred sites, such as the Great Pyramid of Egypt. The controversy over tuning still rages, with proponents of A432 or C256 as being more natural tunings than the current standard.

A major triad is composed of a Root, a Third, and a Fifth and can be formed by using a recurrence relation similar to that of the Fibonacci numbers using note frequencies. If we start with middle C (264 Hz) we get:

264+264=528 (C an octave higher)
264+528=792 (G)
528+729=1320(E)

These three notes, C, E and G form the triad of C major. Although the frequencies of the notes obtained are from three different octaves, it can be seen that the C, E and G families are related to each other by summations of frequencies.

Remembering that the musical ratios discovered by Pythagoras are the same ratios of the Fibonacci sequence, let's simply take a number out of the Fibonacci sequence and its successor and we will get the musical ratio found by Pythagoras.

The Fibonacci sequence is the sequence that gives us beautiful harmonics in music. The Diatonic scale is not the only musical scale, there are many more; in fact no piano today is tuned in the Diatonic scale. But the principle relation between harmonics in music and mathematical progressions of the Fibonacci sequence is real.

Now let's pretend that we've tuned a piano in the Diatonic scale and that we have extended the piano's keyboard with keys to provide for 49 octaves!

But suppose that we could actually play on this piano. When we play the notes in the last two highest octaves, the keys on the furthermost right side of this piano will correspond with the frequencies of the colours of light!

There are 7 keys in the highest octave that are the frequencies of the 7 primary colours of the spectrum of light, the 7 colours of the rainbow!

So not only does the Fibonacci sequence define the ratios of harmonics in sound but also in the electromagnetic spectrum of light, it defines the 7 colours of the rainbow!

OCTAVE	NOTE	COLOUR
	F	Infra-Red
	G	Red
48	A	Orange-yellow
	B	Yellow-green
	C	Green
	D	Green-blue
49	E	Blue-violet
	F	Violet
	G	Ultraviolet

Many musicians, like Beethoven, Mozart, Chopin, Bartók, Schubert and Debussy, used the Fibonacci sequence and the Golden Mean ratio deliberately not in the notes but in the composition itself. For instance, Beethoven used the Golden Mean in his famous *Fifth Symphony*. His famous opening motto not only appears on the first and the last bar of the symphony but also on the bar that represents the exact Golden mean point of his symphony! Bela Bartók used both the Golden Mean and the Fibonacci sequence deliberately in his compositions using the measures 5, 8, 13, 21, 34, 55 and 89 to introduce new instruments such as strings, cellos, percussion etc.

In order to provide an effective approach of Fibonacci sequence and Golden mean, let's come back for a while a few pages ago. The reader will remember that Fibonacci set out to determine how fast rabbits would multiply, given certain mathematical assumptions: a rabbit couple could reproduce once a month beginning at the age of two months, bearing a litter of one male and one female, and no rabbits died. What does this rabbit formula have to do with music? A lot! If we only substitute $x0= 2$ and $x1 = 5$ for the first two terms, we get the series 2, 5, 7, 12, 19, 31, 50..., which bears an important relationship to the structure of musical scales. Any musician will recognize 5, 7 and 12 as the numbers of pitches per octave in pentatonic, diatonic and chromatic scales; and also as the number of black keys, white keys and keys per octave of the traditional musical keyboard.

Now let's see how these numbers build musical structures. The simplest musical interval is the octave, a 2/1 frequency ratio. The next simplest are the fifth, a 3/2 ratio (more or less, in various tunings) and its inversion, the fourth (4/3, more or less).

The numbers in the musical Fibonacci series 2, 5, 7, 12, 19... all are generated by increasingly long series of musical fourths and fifths, as Sir

James Jeans described and shown in the table below.

Scale no.	Calculation	Number of Intervals	Series of musical fifths
1	2 + 0 =	2	F-C (G)
2	5 + 0 =	5	F-C-G-D-A- (E)
3	5 + 2 =	7	F-C-G-D-A-E-B-(F#)
4	7 + 5 =	12	F-C-G-D...G#-D#-A#-(E#)
5	12 +7 =	19	F-C-G-D...Gx-Dx-Ax-(Ex)
6	19 + 12 =	31	Gbb-Dbb...Gx-Dx-Ax-(Ex)
AND SO FORTH...			

Our first division of the octave (scale no. 1 in the table) is into a scale of two tones, a fifth apart: say F and C, with a frequency ratio of 3/2. The next fifth after our two tones is a G, and the resulting sequence of two fifths, 3/2 x 3/2, takes us to 9/4 (2.25), which brings us close to an F a musical octave (2/1) higher than our first F. We think of the G as the same as the F, and stop with a 2-tone scale.

With two tones per octave, it is already possible to play music which distinguishes a tonic and dominant – like a typical tympani part of the early Classical era.

We may also lower the fifths to produce a 2-tone equal temperament. In fact, we can play this temperament on any conventional musical instrument by lowering the C of our 2-tone scale by a half tone to B. But assigning different roles such as "tonic" and "dominant" to each of the two pitches of our scale is difficult. The intervals between them are equal, and so we can't tell which pitch has which role.

Now if we prolong the series of fifths, F-C-G-D-A-(E), the E at the end is close to F again. If we leave the fifths mathematically exact, we can now play pentatonic music ("Mama makes shortnin', shortnin bread...") in one key signature, the way we do on the black keys of any conventional keyboard instrument. As you can see by looking at the black keys, the pentatonic scale consists of groups of three and two pitches separated by two larger steps. This pattern repeats in every octave, allowing us to identify the role of the tones of a pentatonic scale.

But suppose that we raise all of the fifths a little, until the final E is at the same pitch as F. In this way, we construct a 5-tone equal temperament. We can't play this temperament on a regular keyboard, but we can play it on any synthesizer which lets us set nonstandard intervals: set the semitone or octave interval for 2.4 times the standard one (or 1.2 times and play on alternate keys). The resulting scale will sound somewhat out of tune to our ears which are used to standard 12-tone equal temperament, but its melodic and harmonic properties are clear enough. It is not only a theoretical temperament; it is the standard Javanese tuning called 'slendro'.

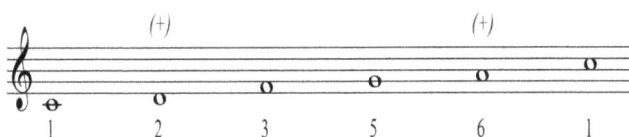

In the 5-tone temperament, we can distinguish tonic and dominant of 2-tone scales and modulate freely among five key signatures – but pentatonic melodies do not work. Even though there are five pitches per octave in this scale, ordinary pentatonic music sounds oddly rootless – we can't determine the key-note. With five equal intervals, there is no differentiation between wide and narrow intervals to identify the pentatonic key signature. This is the same problem we had earlier in distinguishing the tonic and dominant in our 2-tone temperament.

Now that we have established the first two terms of our Fibonacci series, succeeding terms follow logically. Each new, extended series of fifths is the sum of the previous two. The reason for this not the same as for the numbers of Fibonacci's rabbits, but is just as simple: since sequences of two or five fifths approximate whole numbers of octaves, sums of these numbers of fifths also approximate whole numbers of octaves and allow us to close a circle of fifths by filling in the wider steps in the scale, which the earlier series of fifths built. So now let's increase the number of tones per octave, just as Fibonacci did with his rabbit population.

Continuing from 5 on to 7, the series F-C-G-D-A-E-B-(F#) once again brings us close to F. If we leave the fifths exact, we can now play 7-tone diatonic music (like playing on the white keys of the piano), in one key. We can also play 2-and 5-tone music.

If, on the other hand, we lower all of the fifths of our 7-tone scale a little, we arrive at a 7-tone equal temperament. Set the semitone or octave on a synthesizer to 1.7142 (that's 12/7) times standard to play in this temperament. In a 7-tone temperament, we can play in the 2 and 5 tone scales and also play any ordinary pentatonic music with full freedom of modulation in 7 keys.

The 7-tone temperament is not just a theoretical construction. It is the standard tuning used in traditional Siamese music. One might think that, with 7 tones, standard diatonic music in this temperament could be played. But if we try, it sounds oddly rootless! Though we have the seven pitches needed to play diatonic music, the intervals between them are all the same. There is no distinction between large and small intervals to show us what step of the musical scale we are on; the same problem we had playing pentatonic music in the 5-tone temperament in the previous step of our experiment, or 2-tone music in the step before that.

Next, we proceed to the series of 12 fifths, F-C-G-D-A-E-B-F#-C#-G#-D#-A#-(E#). If we lower all of the fifths very slightly, we arrive at our familiar 12-tone equally-tempered tuning. Now we can play all of the music we played in the earlier 2, 5 and 7-tone scales, and we can also play diatonic music using 7-tone scales with full freedom of modulation through 12 keys.

The progression from 7 to 12 tones occurred in European music between the Middle Ages and the Baroque era. Composers have explored the potential of the 12-tone scale over several centuries, and these explorations have culminated in the highly chromatic music of the later Romantic era and "atonal" music of the 20th century.

The term "atonal" reflects the oddly rootless quality of music that moves freely among all 12 of the tones of the scale. Each new temperament generated by extending the series of fifths encompasses the melodic and harmonic possibilities of all of the earlier ones. The mathematical logic of this progression of equal temperaments, and the way it generates new musical possibilities at each step, lead us to ask "what if we went on to the next step of this progression, a 19-tone temperament?"

Another problem is that a practical keyboard to play in a 19-tone temperament does not evolve simply from the traditional keyboard.

A 19-tone keyboard based on the traditional keyboard would have pairs of black keys (Db and C#, Eb and D#, etc.), and an additional black key between the semitone intervals E-F and B-C.

Every diatonic semitone would, then, become a two-step interval, and every diatonic whole tone a three-step interval. The octaves would have to be lengthened to make room for the fingers, with all of the additional keys.

An alternative, favored by Yasser, would be exchange the positions of the black and white keys, front to rear. This keyboard might be somewhat easier to play, but it would still have long octaves and require difficult re-learning.

Another fundamental reason that the 19-tone system has not developed naturally out of the 12-tone system is that the 12-tone system works rather well. The 2, 5, and 7-tone systems which lead up to the 12-tone system have very impure fifths. The fifths in the 12-tone system are quite good.

But going from 12 to 19 tones requires that we make the fifths worse rather than better.

In 19-tone, the minor third is very pure but the major third, though more harmonious than in the 12-tone temperament, is slightly flat, compromising the melodic role of the leading tone.

We should also hope that a system with more than 12 tones would provide good approximations to additional harmonic intervals used in non-western and experimental music (and discussed by Yasser), but the 19-tone system does poorly at this. The 19-tone scale is, for example, not capable of distinguishing between the 7th and 11th harmonics, or of distinguishing the 11th from the augmented fourth.

The 7-tone scales in the 12-tone system approach the limit of what the human mind can assimilate. The rule of "seven plus or minus two" in sensory psychology states that for any sensory continuum, humans describe between five and nine different categories: to give an example, we describe the gray scale using the categories white, off-white, light gray, medium gray, dark gray, near black and black. Though we can discriminate more shades of gray when they are placed side by side for comparison, we do not give names to them, or use the discrimination between them as part of a conceptual structure based on unaided observation and memory.

The musical octave is regarded by sensory psychologists as a continuum like the gray scale, and it follows that 12 distinct pitch classes may be more than we can easily assimilate as elements of a musical structure.

Historically, the evolution toward a 19-tone scale would in fact have succeeded if not for the problems discussed here. The mean-tone temperament used from the late Renaissance through the early Classical era had unequal semitones; it is possible to play Yasser's theoretical 12-tone scale in one key signature on any keyboard instrument tuned in the mean-tone temperament. Not only this, many keyboard instruments, especially organs, had extra keys – for example, separate keys for Eb and D#. The extra keys let the instruments play in several more key signatures than a standard 12-tone keyboard and still avoid the discordant "wolf fifth" which resulted from the mean tone series of fifths' not closing at 12. Handel, among others, had an organ with such a keyboard. The logical culmination of such keyboards with doubled sharps and flats would have been a 19-tone system.

But unlike the transition from the 7-tone to the 12-tone keyboard, the transition to 19 tones never occurred. Instead, 12-tone equal temperament gradually replaced mean-tone temperament beginning around 1700 AD and culminating around 1850 AD.

Suppose, however, that we leap past the 19-tone temperament and examine the next step of our Fibonacci series, with 31 tones.

This temperament turns out to be extremely close to the historical mean-tone temperament, with major thirds that are nearly pure.

In addition, it gives a nearly perfect natural seventh, and a natural 11th which is slightly flat, but distinct from the augmented fourth.

If we put aside the idea of a 12 or 19-tone diatonic scale and regard the 31-tone tuning primarily as a tool to improve the intonation of traditional scales and intervals, then it looks like a sensible idea.

That said – this introduction is right and proper to contextualize the contents of this chapter – it is not well known that Mozart was fascinated by mathematics, Numerology and especially Gematria (*see* pag. 103). Chances are excellent that he knew of the Golden Section and its reputation for conferring elegance on structures – even musical compositions.

Several scholars studied the relationship between art and mathematics and claim that in art most of us are attracted to symmetry spiced by some elements of surprise, and that combination is the essence of Mozart's music. It may indeed be noted that this symmetry and harmony is the very essence of mathematics.

Thus the connection between music and mathematics has always found fertile ground in the works of Mozart!

According to his sister, Nannerl, Wolfgang "talked of nothing, thought of nothing but figures" during his school days. Moreover, he jotted mathematical equations in the margins of some of his compositions, including *Fantasia and Fugue in C Major* – K394, where he calculated his odds of winning a lottery. Although these equations did not relate to his music, they do suggest an attraction to mathematics.

The structure of Mozart's music attracted the attention of John F. Putz, a mathematician at Alma College. "My son, who is a composer and pianist, told me that Mozart's piano sonatas are divided into two distinct sections," Putz recalls. "I knew that Mozart's music is highly regarded for its elegant proportions, among other things, so I thought it would be interesting to check whether the divisions Mozart used were very close to golden-section divisions."

In the October 1995 issue of Mathematics Magazine (68(4):275-282), Putz described his investigation of whether the golden ratio appears in Mozart's piano sonatas. According to Putz:

> In Mozart's time, the sonata-form movement was conceived in two parts: the Ex-

position in which the musical theme is introduced, and the Development and Recapitulation in which the theme is developed and revisited... It is this separation into two distinct sections [...] [that] gives cause to wonder how Mozart apportioned these works.

That is, did Mozart divide his sonatas according to the golden ratio, with the exposition as the shorter segment and the development and recapitulation as the longer one?

The first two parts of the *Sonata No. 1 in C Major*, 279 I and 279 II, are perfectly divided into the Golden Ratio: 279 I has 100 measures, with the exposition 38 measures long and the development/recapitulation is 62 measures long. For the natural numbers, 62 could not be closer to 100φ. In 279 II, the 74 measures are divided into 28 and 46 measures, respectively. This again could not be closer to the golden ratio. However, for the third part of K. 279 is not exactly divided into the golden section.

The next figure is a scatter plot of b against $a+b$ with the line $y=\phi x$ and the regression line.

An equally good approximation to the golden section exists in the second movement of that sonata. The third movement, however, deviates from the golden section.

A clear answer to Putz's question required looking at more than one sonata. So Putz examined 29 movements from Mozart's piano sonatas-the ones that consist of two distinct sections. Then he plotted the number of measures in the development and recapitulation versus the total number of measures in each movement, which is the right side of the golden section equality as given earlier. The results reveal a stunningly straight line – so straight that its correlation coefficient equals 0.99, or nearly the 1.00 of a perfectly straight line. Moreover, the distribution of the ratios of the number of measures in the development and recapitulation to the total number of measures in each movement lies tightly packed and virtually on top of the golden ratio.

Although those results might seem like solid evidence that Mozart did use the golden ratio when he divided the sections of his piano sonatas, Putz knew that another comparison must be made. If Mozart used the golden section, then the other ratio from the golden – section equality – in this case, the ratio of the number of measures in an exposition to those in the recapitulation and development – should also equal the golden ratio.

A plot of those measurements also produces a very straight line, but one with a lower correlation coefficient of 0.938, which Putz interpreted as "somewhat less goodness of fit."

In addition, the distribution of the ratios of the number of measures in the expositions to those in the recapitulation and development peaks near the golden ratio of 0.618, but it also covers a considerable spread, ranging from 0.534 to 0.833.

The results from the two analyses seemingly conflict. The first analysis suggests that Mozart probably did use the golden section, but the variability in the ratios from the second analysis suggests that he did not use the golden section. That disagreement, however, did not surprise Putz, who wrote that the mathematics behind the golden section predict that "what we have observed in these data is true for all data..." That is, the ratio of the longer segment to the overall length is always closer to the golden ratio than is the ratio of the shorter segment to the longer one.

As such, Putz concentrated on the distribution of the latter ratio as constrained by sonata form, and the spread in the distribution of ratios from that analysis suggests that Mozart

did not apply the golden section to his piano
sonatas.

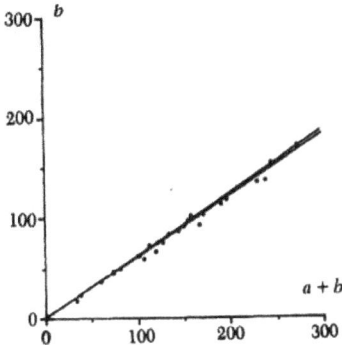

If $\frac{b}{a+b}$ is near the ratio, then $\frac{a}{b}$ should also
be near the ratio. The next figure is a plot of a
against b with $y=\phi x$ and the regression line
plotted as well. We can see that there appears
to be less linearity.

The following figure is the frequency distribution of $\frac{a}{b}$. Here, we see that there is less evidence for the centrality of φ.

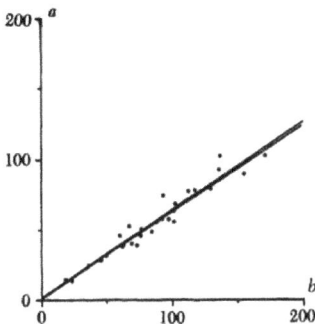

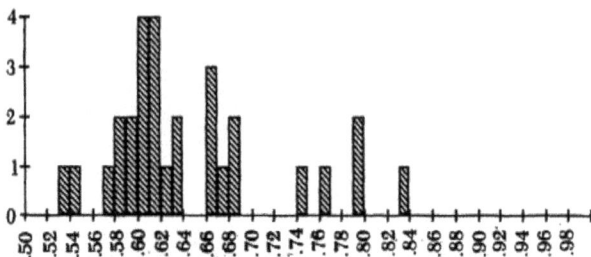

Putz states that there is a theorem that *ba+b* is always nearer to φ than ab.

In the end, we may never know if Mozart composed his sonatas, even in part, from equations. "We must remember," Putz writes, "that these sonatas are the work of a genius, and one who loved to play with numbers. Mozart may have known of the golden section and used it."

Nevertheless, Putz thinks that the considerable variation in the data "suggests otherwise". In any case, Mozart did create divine divisions in his piano sonatas-making the interplay of sections shine like sunlight. Yet he apparently timed those divisions with his mind – not with math, or at least not with the golden section.[93]

Let's analyse other examples.

---

[93] MAY MIKE, *"Did Mozart Use the Golden Section?"*, American Scientist, 84:118, 1996.

In *Don Giovanni*, Leporello's "catalogue aria" first recites the libertine's conquests as adding up to an unstated 1,062 (640 in Italy, 231 in Germany, 100 in France and 91 in Turkey) then adds to this sum 1,003 conquests in Spain, making a total of 2065. The difference between the partial sums is 59 (1062-1003) and dividing the full sum (1062+1003) by the difference between the partial sums is 35, which may or may not be significant.

In his earlier *Le nozze di Figaro*, Figaro counts out in his footsteps the measure of his imagined quarters to be shared with Susanna: 5, 10, 20, 30, 36, 43, the sum of which is 144 or 12 squared, as others like de Sautoy have pointed out, again noting it may not have any additional meaning, although coincidence seems unlike Mozart.

Mario Livio, author and mathematical astrophysicist, also highlights the mathematical symmetry of Mozart's music, especially his "symmetry under translation" and the sheer intellectuality of his music. Livio discusses Mozart's *Musical Dice Game Minuet* of 16 measures with the choice of one of 11 possible variations in measure endings from random selection, each possibility selected by a roll of two dice, with literally trillions of possible mirror combinations.[94]

Contemporary musician composers like Karl Ditters von Dittersdorf (1739-99) acknowledged of Mozart that "[...] he is undoubtedly one of the greatest of original geniuses and I have never known any other composer to possess such an amazing wealth of ideas."[95]

Mozart also loved writing musical themes from observing the bounces of a billiard ball off table corners and like phenomena and also was extremely adept at writing musical palindromes and an almost infinite variety of musical games as well as playful musical and literary punning.

When examining some of his scores, for example, his *Symphony K40 in G minor*, the developments and inversions of his musical themes are like contrapuntal and antiphonal number games between flute and violins, especially in bridging passages between measures 119 and following, again in fugal

---

[94] *"The Mathematics of Mozart's Music"* transcript. All Things Considered – NPR. Jan. 26 2006. *Also see* Mario Livio, *The Golden Ratio: The Story of Phi*. Random House, 2003, 187-8.

[95] Cf. Alfred Hutchings, *Mozart: The Man, The Musician*. Schirmer Books, 1976, 84.

passages beginning in measures 150 ff & 160-220 in the first movement.[96] Mozart's music often looks deceptively simple, yet is anything but, however rewarding its complementary visual symmetry. As playfully childlike by nature he remained through life, he was not merely an automaton who received his music thoughtlessly.[97]

It has long been established that Mozart carried much of his music in his head before ever committing it to any manuscript. Livio concludes that one of the elements we love most about Mozart is the playful brilliance of his musical inventiveness that balances "predictability versus surprise", a mathematical economy of variability that is exquisitely pleasing to the astute listener but may be also profoundly appreciated when the mind may not be consciously concentrating on the music itself. How much of this was intended by Mozart is impossible to know, but this is one of the ways genius works even intuitively, and

---

[96] BONAVIA F. - GORDON JACOB, notes. *Mozart, Symphony 40 in G Minor.* Penguin Scores I – 2/6, Harmondsworth, Middlesex,England, 1949,13-15 (G. Jacob notes); also score 12-13, 16-20.
[97] PATRICK HUNT, *Amadeus* in *Masterplots*, Amenya, NY: Salem Press, 2010, vol. 1, 4th ed., 160 & ff.

what is intuition but the natural expression of the deepest level of the mind at work independent of effort? As Hutchings pointed out, Mozart's humility toward his own mortality despite his awareness of his musical uniqueness,[98] it may be this similar paradox floating between ephemerality and eternity as part of the timelessness that draws us to Mozart's genius: his capacity for complexity. Ultimately, Mozart would probably agree on this: music is mathematics you can hear!

Mozart's life brings to us some unique characteristics of geniuses in the field of music and mathematics. While the best works of a poet are often later in life, the best works of a musician or a mathematician seems to be generally when they are young. Statistically speaking, performing musicians and mathematicians tend to mature young, and music and mathematics both tend to exhibit child genius more so than other disciplines.

The mystic connection between music and mathematics brings to us the question: does one need to have a good mathematical brain to develop excellence in music, and the vice versa? Or do the musical and mathematical

---

[98] Cf. Alfred Hutchings, *Mozart: The Man, The Musician.* Schirmer Books, 1976, 99.

brains or minds have the same roots. In fact it can be argued that the roots of mathematics are closely connected with those of music. The rational structure of mathematics is implicitly aesthetic, given its properties of order and harmony, and in this sense it is musical, even though there is no transmission of sound. By the same token, music – even though there are no explicit digits or other mathematical signs in it – is implicitly mathematical through its amplitude, frequency, quality, rhythm, melody, form and style.

As a matter of fact, we do not have to go too far deep into any mathematical analysis to believe that music has some affinity with mathematics.

Many mathematicians are also good musicians. The life and works of the scientist, Albert Einstein throws much light in this direction. The picture of Einstein conjures in us an image of a genius who discovered the formula $E=MC^2$ on one hand and who plays the violin with the other. In his real life, Einstein was fascinated by Mozart and sensed an affinity between their creative processes, as well as their histories. Einstein once said that while Beethoven created his music, Mozart's "was so pure that it seemed to have been ever-present in the universe, waiting to be discovered by the master." Einstein believed much the same of physics, that beyond observations and theory lay the music of the spheres — which, he wrote, revealed a "pre-established harmony" exhibiting stunning symmetries. The laws of nature, such as those of relativity theory, were waiting to be plucked out of the cosmos by someone with a sympathetic ear. Thus it was mainly to "pure thought" and less to laborious calculation, which Einstein attributed his theories.

For 250 years now, artists, writers and musicians have been tinkering with Mozart's music and legend, yet Mozart remains as untouched by it all as the day he strolled into Vienna.

From operas to musical ditties whistled by first-graders, Mozart's music remains a touchstone for humanity and a gateway to the realm of angels. Musicologists may mull over the reasons for that, but the public has already voted: Mozart remains a genius who wrote music that thrilled the head and the heart. Like the great classical novels of the past, his music is both popular and immortal. As the critics would say, it is music that seems to "lie beyond making." This reminds us of the famous saying by Rabindranath Tegore who said, *Songit jinista gogoner* (The music stuff is of the haven).

"Music," Mozart once wrote, "even in situations of the greatest horror, should never be painful to the ear but should flatter and charm it, and thereby always remains music." Such a creed would eventually prompted Goethe to declare:

Mozart should have written 'Faust'.[99]

---

[99] GOETHE J.W., *Conversations of Goethe with Eckermann and Soret*, English translation: John Oxenford, Cambridge: Cambridge University Press, 2011.

Bibliography

ABERT HERMANN, *W. A. Mozart*, Cliff Eisen (ed.), Stewart Spencer (trans.), New Haven: Yale University Press, 2007

ANDERSON EMILY, *Mozart's Letters: An Illustrated Selection*, Boston: Little, Brown and Company, 1990
— *The letters of Mozart and his family*, New York: W.W. Norton & CO., 1985

BARRY BARBARA R., *The Philosopher's Stone: Essays in the Transformation of Musical Structure*, Hillsdale, NY: Pendragon Press, 2000

BIANCOLLI LOUIS, *The Mozart Handbook: a Guide to the Man and His Music*, Cleveland: Word Publishing Company, 1954

BOROWITZ ALBERT, *Salieri and the "Murder" of Mozart*, The Musical Quarterly 59 (2), April 1973

BRAUENBEHRENS VOLKMAR, *Salieri: un musicista all'ombra di Mozart*, translation by Silvia Tuja, Scandicci: La Nuova Italia, 1997

— *Mozart in Vienna*, New York: Grove and Weidenfeld, 1990

BRIDGETT D.J. - CUEVAS J., *Effects of listening to Mozart and Bach on the performance of a mathematical test*", Perceptual and motor skills, 90, 2000

BRION MARCEL, *Daily life in the Vienna of Mozart and Schubert*, Trans. by Jean Stewart, New York: The Macmillan Company, 1962

BROPHY BRIGID, *Mozart the Dramatist: the value of his operas to him, to his age, and to us*, revised edition, New York: Da Capo Press, 1988

BURGESS ANTHONY, *On Mozart: A Paean for Wolfgang*, New York: Tecknor & Fields, 1991

BURK JOHN N., *Mozart and his Music*, New York: Random House, 1959

CAIRNS DAVID, *"A Vision of Reconciliation" in The Magic Flute*, ed. N. John, London: John Calder, 1980, 2nd edition
— *Mozart and his operas*, Berkeley: University of California Press, 2006

CAMPBELL DON, *The Mozart Effect for Children Awakening Your Child's Mind, Health and Creativity with Music*, New York: HarperCollins Publishers Inc, 2000
— *The Mozart effect: tapping the power of music to heal the body, strengthen the mind, and unlock the creative spirit*, New York: Avon Books, 1997

CARR FRANCIS, *Mozart & Constanze*, New York: Avon Books, 1985

CASINI CLAUDIO, *Amadeus. Vita di Mozart*, Rimini: Rusconi, 1990

CONNOLLY KATE, *Sewage plant plays Mozart to stimulate microbes* (2 June 2010), The Guardian, Retrieved 8 April 2011

COWELL STEPHANIE, *Marrying Mozart: a novel*, New York: Penguin Books 2004

DAVENPORT MARCIA, *Mozart*, New York: Charles Scribner's sons, 1932

DAVID J. BUCH, *Magic Flutes and Enchanted Forests*, Chicago: The University of Chicago Press, 2008

DAVIES PETER J., *Mozart in Person: His Character and Health*, New York: Greenwood Press, 1989

DENT E. J., *Mozart's Operas: A Critical Study*, Oxford: Oxford University Press, 1947, 2nd edition

DEUTSCH OTTO ERICH, *Mozart: A Documentary Biography*, Stanford: Stanford University Press, 1965

DRAKE JR, *Mozart's chronic subdural hematoma*, Neurology 43 (11): 2400–3, ME, 1993

EINSTEIN ALFRED, *Mozart: his character, his work*, Trans. By Stewart Spencer, New York: Penguin Books, 2006

EISEN CLIFF - KEEFE SIMON P., *The Cambridge Mozart Encyclopedia*, Cambridge: Cambridge University Press, 2006

EISEN CLIFF, *Mozart: a life in letters*, Trans. By Stewart Spencer, New York: Penguin Books, 2006

EVÉNEMENT MÉDIA, *Wolfgang Amadeus Mozart 1791-1991: the official International Magazine of the Mozart Bicentenary*, Salzburg, Austria: Evénement Média, 1991

GLOVER JANE, *Mozart's Women: His Family, His Friends, His Music*, London: Macmillan, 2005

GOETHE J.W., *Conversations of Goethe with Eckermann and Soret*, English translation by John Oxenford, Cambridge: Cambridge University Press, 2011

GOODE ERICA, *Mozart For Baby? Some Say, Maybe Not*, The New York Times, 1999-08-03 p. f1: Rauscher, "The money could be better spent on music education programs"

GRANT W.B. - PILS S., *Vitamin D deficiency contributed to Mozart's death*, Medical Problems of Performing Artists, 26 N2, 117, 2011

GRAZIANO A.B. - PETERSON M. - SHAW G.L., *Enhanced learning of proportional maths through music training and spatial-temporal reasoning*, Neurol Res 1999, 21: 139-52

GUTMAN ROBERT, *Mozart: A Cultural Biography*, London: Harcourt Brace, 2000

HALLIWELL RUTH, *The Mozart Family: Four Lives in a Social Context*, New York: Clarendon Press, 1998

HEARTZ DANIEL, *Music in European Capitals: The Galant Style, 1720-1780*, (1St ed.), New York: W. W. Norton & Company, 2003
— *Haydn, Mozart, and the Viennese School, 1740-1780*, New York: W. W. Norton, 1995

HILDESHEIMER WOLFGANG, *Mozart*, English translation by Marion Faber, New York: Farrar Straus Groux, 1982

HOLMES EDWARD, *Life of Mozart, Including His Correspondence*, New York: Harper & Brothers, 1854

HOWARD CHANDLER ROBBINS LANDON, *1791: Mozart's Last Year*. London: Flamingo, 1990

HUGHES J. - DAABOUL Y. - FINO J. - SHAW G., *The Mozart effect on epileptiform activity*, Clin Electroencephalogr, 29 (3), 109-19, 1998, Retrieved December 3, 2007, from Pubmed Database

HUGHES JR - FINO JJ - MELYN MA, *Is there a chronic change of the "Mozart effect" on epileptiform activity? A case study, Clin Electroencephalogr* 1999; 30: 44-5

HUGHES JR, FINO JJ, *The Mozart effect: distinctive aspects of the music — a clue to brain coding?, Clin Electroencephalogr* 2000;31: 94-103

HUSAIN G., THOMPSON W.F., SCHELLENBERG, E.G., *Effects of musical tempo and mode on arousal, mood, and spatial abilities: Re-examination of the "Mozart effect"*, 2002, Music Perception, 20

HUTCHINGS ALFRED, *Mozart: The Man, The Musician*, New York: G. Schirmer Inc., 1976

Improved maze learning through early music exposure in rats. Neurol. Res. (National Center for Biotechnology Information) 20 (5): 427–32. July 1998

IRVING JOHN, *Mozart's Piano Sonatas: Contexts, Sources, Style*, Cambridge: Cambridge University Press, 1997

JAHN OTTO, *Life of Mozart*, Trans. By Pauline D. Townsend, Preface by George Grove, London: Novello, Ewer & Company, 1882

Journal of the Royal Society of Medicine, Volume 80, November 1987

JULIAN RUSHTON, *Mozart: His Life And Works*, New York, NY: Oxford University Press, 2005

LIGEOIS-CHAUVEL C. - PERETZ I. - BABAI M. *et al., Contribution of different cortical areas in the temporal lobes to music processing*, *Brain* 1998; 121: 1853-67

MARIO LIVIO, *The Golden Ratio: The Story of Phi*, New York: Random House, 2003

MAY MIKE, *"Did Mozart Use the Golden Section?"*, American Scientist, 84:118, 1996

MAYNARD SOLOMON, *Mozart: A Life*, New York: HarperCollins Publishers, 1995

MCKELVIE P. – JASON LOW J., *Listening to Mozart does not improve children's spatial ability: Final curtains for the Mozart effect*, 2002, British Journal of Developmental Psychology, 20

MEDICAL JOURNAL ARTICLE: *What Killed Mozart?*, by Jan V. Hirschmann, MD, in Archives of Internal Medicine, Volume 161, June 2001

MELLET E. - TZOURIO N. - CRIVELLO F. *et al., Functional anatomy of spatial imagery generated from verbal instructions*, J Neurosci 1996; 16: 6504-12

MELOGRANI PIERO, *Wolfgang Amadeus Mozart: A Biography*, Trans. by Lydia G. Cochrane (Original title, *La vita e il tempo di Wolfgang Amadeus Mozart*, 2003), Chicago: University of Chicago Press, 2007

MILNES RODNEY, *'Singspiel and Symbolism' in The Magic Flute*, ed. N. John, London: John Calder, 1980, 2nd edition

MÖRIKE EDUARD F., *Mozart on the way to Prague*, ill. By Eliane Bonabel, Translation and Introduction by Walter and Catherine Alison Phillips, New York: Pantheon, 1947

Mozart W.A., *Die Zauberflotescore*, London: Barenreiter, 1960

Nakamura S. - Sadato N. - Oohashi T. *et al., Analysis of music-brain interaction with simultaneous measurement of regional blood flow and electroencephalogram beta rhythm in human subjects*, Neurosci Lett 1999, 275: 222-6

Nettl Paul, *Mozart and Masonry*, New York: Philosophical Library, 1957

Newman J. - Rosenback J.H. - Burns I.L. *et al. An experimental test of "the Mozart effect": does listening to his music improve spatial ability?*, Percept Motor Skills 1995, 81: 1379-87

Nohl Ludwig, *The life of Mozart*, Trans. By Lady Wallace, London: Longmans, Green and Company, 1880

Norbert Elias, *Mozart: portrait of a genius*, edited by Michael Schröter, Translation by Edmund Jephcott, Berkeley and Los Angeles: University of California Press, 1993

OTTO ERICH DEUTSCH, *Mozart. A documentary bibliography*, Stanford, California: Stanford University Press, 1965

PATRICK HUNT, *Amadeus* in *Masterplots*, Amenya, NY: Salem Press, 2010, vol. 1, 4th ed.

PLATEL H. - PRICE C. - BARON J.C. *et al., The structural components of music perception: a functional anatomical study*, Brain 1997, 120: 229-43

RAU HERIBERT, *Mozart: a Biographical Romance*, Trans. By E.R. Sill, Boston: Oliver Ditson & Company, 1870

RAUSCHER FH - ROBINSON KD - JENS JJ, *Improved maze learning through early music exposure in rats*, Neurol Res 1998, 20: 427-32

RAUSCHER F.H. - SHAW G.L. - KY K.N., *Listening to Mozart enhances spatial-temporal reasoning: toward a neurophysiological basis*, Neurosci Lett 1995, 185: 44-7
  — *Music and spatial task performance*, Nature, 1993;365: 611 Chabris, *Prelude or requiem for the `Mozart effect'?*, Nature, 1999, 400: 826-7

RAUSCHER F.H. - SHAW G.L. - LEVINE L.J. *et al., Music training causes longterm enhancement of preschool children's spatial-temporal reasoning, Neurol Res* 1997, 19: 2-8

RIDEOUT B.E. - DOUGHERTY S. - WERNERT L., *Effect of music on spatial performance: a test of generality, Percept Motor Skills* 1998, 86: 512-14

RIDEOUT B.E. - LAUBACH C.M., *EEG correlates of enhanced spatial performance following exposure to music, Percept Motor Skills* 1996, 82: 427-32

ROSEN CHARLES, *The Classical Style: Haydn, Mozart, Beethoven* (2nd ed.), New York: W. W. Norton & Company, 1998

ROSSELLI JOHN, *The life of Mozart*, New York: Cambridge UP, 1998

SACKS OLIVER, *Musicophilia Tales of Music and the Brain*, Toronto: Random House of Canada, 2007

SADIE STANLEY, *Mozart: the early years, 1756-1781*, New York: W.W. Norton & CO., 2006

— *The New Grove Dictionary of Opera*, New York: Grove's Dictionaries of Music Inc., 1998

SARNTHEIN J. - VON STEIN A. - RAPPELSBERGER P. *et al., Persistent patterns of brain activity: an EEG coherence study of the positive effect of music on spatial-temporal reasoning. Neurol Res* 1997, 19: 107-16

SCHELLENBERG E.G. - HALLAM S., *Music listening and cognitive abilities in 10 and 11 year olds: The Blur effect*, Annals of The New York Academy of Sciences, 1060, 2005

SCHENK ERICH, *Mozart and his times*, New York: Knopf, 1959

SELBY AGNES, *Constanze: Mozart's beloved*, Sydney: Turton & Armstrong, 1999

SOLOMON MAYNARD, *Mozart: A Life*, Hammersmith: Harper Collins, 1995

STAFFORD WILLIAM, *The Mozart Myths: A Critical Reassessment*, Sanford: Stanford University Press, 1991

STEELE K. M. - DALLA BELLA S. – PERETZ I. – DUNLOP T. - DAWE L. A. – HUMPHREY G. K. – SHANNON R. A. - KIRBY JR. J. L. – OLMSYEAD C. G., *Prelude or requiem for the 'Mozart effect'?* NATURE, 1999, 400, 827

STEPTOE ANDREW, *The Mozart-Da Ponte Operas: The Cultural and Musical Background to Le nozze di Figaro, Don Giovanni, and Così fan tutte*, Oxford: Clarendon Press, 1990

The Cambridge Mozart Encyclopedia, ed. by Cliff Eisen and Simon P. Keefe, Cambridge: Cambridge University Press, 2006

The Mathematics of Mozart's Music transcript. *All Things Considered – NPR.* Jan. 26 2006

THERIVEL WILLIAM A., *Creative genius and the GAM theory of personality: Why Mozart and not Salieri?, Journal of Social Behavior & Personality* 13.2 (1998): 201-34. EBSCO. Web. 15 Oct. 2009

THOMPSON W.F., SCHELLENBERG E.G., HUSAIN G., *Mood, arousal, and the Mozart effect.* Psychological Science, 12(3), 2001

THOMSON KATHERINE, *The Masonic Thread in Mozart*, London: Lawrence and Wishart, 1977

TILL NICHOLAS, *Mozart and the Enlightenment: Truth, Virtue and Beauty in Mozart's Operas*, New York: W.W. Norton, 1995

VIGELAND CARL, *The Mostly Mozart Guide to Mozart.*, Hoboken, NJ: John Wiley & Sons, Inc., 2009

WARREN J.D., *Variations on the musical brain, J R Soc Med* 1999, 92: 571-5

WILSON T. - BROWN T., *Re-examination of the effect of Mozart's music on spatial task performance. Journal of Psychology*. 131 (4), 365, 1997, Retrieved December 4, 2007, from EbscoHost Research Databases

www.ingramcontent.com/pod-product-compliance
Lightning Source LLC
Chambersburg PA
CBHW070031100426
42740CB00013B/2657